playing the changes

BASS

A LINEAR APPROACH TO IMPROVISING

Paul Del Nero

Edited by Jonathan Feist

Berklee Media

Vice President: Dave Kusek
Dean of Continuing Education: Debbie Cavalier
Director of Business Affairs: Robert Green
Technology Manager: Mike Serio
Marketing Manager, Berkleemusic: Barry Kelly
Senior Designer: Robert Heath

Berklee Press

Senior Writer/Editor: Jonathan Feist
Production Manager: Shawn Girsberger
Marketing Manager, Berklee Press: Jennifer D'Angora

ISBN-13: 978-0-634-02222-7
ISBN-10: 0-634-02222-9

1140 Boylston Street
Boston, MA 02215-3693 USA
(617) 747-2146

Visit Berklee Press Online at
www.berkleepress.com

DISTRIBUTED BY

HAL•LEONARD®
CORPORATION
7777 W. BLUEMOUND RD. P.O. BOX 13819
MILWAUKEE, WISCONSIN 53213

Visit Hal Leonard Online at
www.halleonard.com

Contents

CD Tracks

Paul Del Nero: Bass
Tony Germain: Piano
Bob Tamagni: Drums

Recorded at PBS Recording in Westwood, MA by Peter Kontrimas.

Additional recordings for this book are available on its associated Website: www.playingthechanges.com.

Introduction

This book began as a series of core courses at Berklee College of Music, developed by members of the Ear Training Department. In these classes, jazz improvisation students learn to develop an intuitive, linear sense of improvisation. Some of these techniques have evolved over centuries, and others have been developed fairly recently. As a method for training musicians how to improvise, we have found this approach to be uniquely effective.

This book is intended for musicians who can read traditional notation and chord symbols, have a basic understanding of functional harmony, and have a basic technical capability on their instrument.

The essential idea is that using just a few notes effectively, in an improvisation, leads to great musical freedom and depth of expression. By using a few carefully selected notes, and by listening for where these notes naturally lead, your resulting improvised lines will become more focused and linear, with natural-sounding resolutions.

This type of linear approach can be especially useful to bass players. The bass's usual role in the rhythm section is to outline the chords of the progression—namely, the root motion and secondary chord quality. When it's time to solo, many bass players will continue trying to outline every chord in the progression.

This book is an attempt to break away from that approach to improvising. In our method, note choices are based on modes and *tetrachords* (four-note groups, discussed in lesson 2) that are derived from the chord progression's harmony. Our method for using them will help you to find notes that will be musically effective, easy to remember, and appropriate for your instrument, and it will lead you to many new ideas.

After introducing a few technical concepts in part I, the "Progressions" lessons of part II are each based on a progression from the "jazz standards" repertoire. These patterns of chords are at the heart of many tunes, and there are infinite ways in which they can be varied. Individual chords can have variations, melodies can include notes that go beyond the chords, and distinctive elements in the underlying groove can all lead to countless possibilities. In addition, these progressions may be transposed to any key and played at various tempos. Tunes can be created by combining several of these progressions, in various formal structures. Mastering the ways that notes move over these progressions will therefore help you as you learn new music.

Berklee has used this approach to train thousands of students to develop their musical intuition. It has been refined over many years, and we have found it to be uniquely effective and helpful.

I hope that it helps you to become more expressive and creative in your music making.

Notes about Chord Symbols

Chord symbols don't necessarily include tensions. Tensions may be included in the notated and recorded bass lines and solos.

In this book, minor chords are indicated with the − symbol.

PART I. Getting Oriented

These lessons present strategies for orienting yourself in a progression, as you prepare to solo.

The goal is to develop an *expectation of sound*—an intuitive sense for what harmonies will follow, for what notes will sound good, and for where your chosen notes will lead you, in your improvisations.

Where are you in the tune, and what should you play? The strategies presented here will help you answer these fundamental questions and give you the freedom and the tools to explore the possibilities suggested by the harmony.

Lesson 1. Pitch Axis

A *pitch axis* is a tone common to all chords in a progression, and it can serve to anchor them. Consider this simple progression. What is the pitch axis—the note most important to all chords?

Although there are other common tones, the strong pitch axis here is the tonic note C. When you know this, you can then choose different scales based on it, such as C major (Ionian) or C minor (Aeolian), to use over the respective chords. The axis point, C, persists throughout. Recognizing and hearing this helps simplify the task of determining effective notes for improvisation because all scales in the progression are based on the same tonic.

Next, consider this vamp.

Here, the pitch axis is again the note C. In the CMaj7 chord, C is the tonic and the strongest note. In the F–7 chord, C is the fifth, which is also an important note. While the C major scale (Ionian mode) would work well for improvising over the CMaj7 chord, when the harmony changes to F–7, the C Aeolian scale (mode) becomes a better choice, as it includes the A♭ from the key of F minor. But the pitch axis, C, persists.

Using a pitch axis will help you maintain a point of orientation on your instrument and with your ear. For as long as C remains the axis point, you need only determine which mode of C to use, as the basis for your improvisations.

We will practice using pitch axes throughout this method. In many progressions, the pitch axis shifts. In this method, we use progressions where we can establish a pitch axis that remains the same throughout, so that you have the opportunity to practice using this powerful tool.

Finding Pitch Axes

The starting pitch axis will be the progression's initial key. If the progression modulates and the initial pitch axis remains a common tone to all of the progression's chords, it will continue to be the pitch axis. If the progression modulates to a key where the initial pitch axis is no longer a common tone, a new pitch axis will be in play.

Lesson 2. Tetrachords

Once you know a progression's pitch axis, you can then begin building larger structures to use as note sources, such as tetrachords. A *tetrachord* is simply a group of four notes. For our purposes, we will use the tetrachords that are at either the first four or the last four notes of a scale or mode.

Here is the C major tetrachord, shown with the rest of the C major scale (Ionian mode).

In a chord progression, while the pitch axis may persist over changing harmonies, the tetrachords that will be most effective to use on individual chords may change. Four specific kinds of tetrachords are especially useful to improvisers. They all include whole steps and either one half step or no half steps, and differ only in the placement of the half step.

1. The *major* tetrachord places the half step between notes 3 and 4.

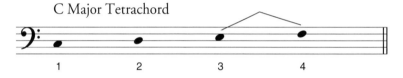

2. The *minor* tetrachord places the half step between notes 2 and 3.

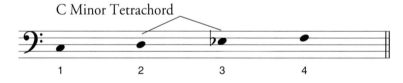

3. The *Phrygian* tetrachord places the half step between notes 1 and 2.

4. The *Lydian* tetrachord does not include any half steps.

These names help us reference the groupings easily, but remembering the placement of the half steps and remembering the sound quality of each tetrachord are what is most important while you are improvising. This ties into the "expectation of sound" and developing an awareness of sound.

These four tetrachord qualities are the building blocks for all seven of the major-scale modes. To review, here are all the modes, with their component tetrachords labeled.

This method explores a linear approach for improvising over chord progressions. Larger intervals should be used more sparingly, within a phrase.

Tetrachords in Improvisation

The next step is to determine which tetrachord notes are stable against the chord and which have tendencies to move to other notes and therefore require special handling. Tetrachord notes that are also chord tones are stable and don't have strong tendencies to move towards other notes. Tetrachord notes that are a half step above chord tones are unstable and will pull downward towards the chord tone, such as F's tendency to move towards E, when played against a CMaj7 chord.

Hearing the tendencies for where each pitch naturally moves will help you choose notes more effectively. To practice this, you will create chord "pads" over which you can practice building your tetrachords, playing each note, in your own tempo, and listening for how it is inclined to resolve. Here's an example of the type of pad you might create to practice improvising on a CMaj7 chord.

Creating Pads

Use a keyboard, sequencer, or software tools to generate your own pads. Just make sure that a single chord sustains for thirty seconds, and that every note of the chord sounds.

On the Web

Chord pads for the exercises in this book are also available for download from Berklee Press. Here's the URL:

www.playingthechanges.com

Beginning in lesson 4, you'll practice listening to a chord and then improvising over it with only the notes of one tetrachord, practicing each chord/tetrachord pair one by one. This will let you hear the tension or release that each note has in relation to the chord pad. It might sound like CD 5. In this example, a C major tetrachord is used to improvise against a CMaj7 chord. As discussed, the non-chord-tone F tends to move to the closest adjacent chord tone of CMaj7, E.

Pad Practice

Let's practice the C major tetrachord over a CMaj7 pad. The tetrachord notes C, D, and E are stable. The note F is inclined towards E. Throughout this method, we notate such tendencies as follows.

C Major Tetrachord

Play CD 4, and practice improvising over the CMaj7 pad using only the notes of the C major tetrachord. Listen to each note, observing the natural inclinations of where the pitches move.

C Major Tetrachord

Often, you will improvise using several tetrachords over the same practice pad. The indicated pitches in the notation may only apply to some of the tetrachords listed. Tetrachords that include one or more of the notes indicated in the notation are set in bold type. If the tetrachord is not in bold, as in "G Major Tetrachord" below, then none of the pitches of that tetrachord require special handling against that harmony. Here, the note F only occurs in the C major tetrachord, so only that label is bold and only that tetrachord requires special handling.

CMaj7

C Major Tetrachord
G Major Tetrachord

Throughout this book, you will use pads similar to CD 4, and practice tetrachords over them. These exercises will strengthen your ear to recognize notes played against harmonies, and will help you to develop your *expectation of sound*—your intuitive sense of what notes and melodic motions will be effective in the music to come. Your ear will guide you through the progression, and you'll hear the natural resting place or end of phrase for your improvised lines.

Singing

Practice singing the tetrachords along with the pads. For an added challenge, sing the tetrachords while you play the root on your bass, rather than singing along with your recording. This will allow you to easily vary the chord order from that of the progression, which is a tremendous benefit and practice technique. You can also use your bass to help correct your pitches, as necessary.

Lesson 3. Modes

A traditional way of setting these tetrachords is by framing them between a low pitch axis on the bottom and a high one on top. This reveals that the C major tetrachord and the G major tetrachord combine to form the C major scale (Ionian mode). Here, the note C is the pitch axis.

Another way to think of this is as two tetrachords extended off a pitch axis, one ascending and the other descending from it.

This illustrates how the pitch axis can bring two different structures together. From it, you can easily create an ascending or descending line, which suggests more flexibility of movement than does the traditional ordering. Grouping the notes within the scale simplifies the process of choosing notes, and it naturally will lead you to many ideas that will help you focus your playing.

Matching Modes to Chords

To choose which mode to use on a given chord, first determine the progression's beginning pitch axis. Then, consider the tones of each chord in the progression, one by one, and how long they are consistently within the same mode.

Here's the first phrase of the chord progression used in "Tune Up," by Miles Davis (some credit Eddie "Cleanhead" Vinson). The pitch axis of this progression is D.

Let's see what mode of D can be derived from these chords. List all the chords' tones, and for the first three chords, you'll get the notes from a D major scale (Ionian mode). D major is therefore the "parent scale" of this region.

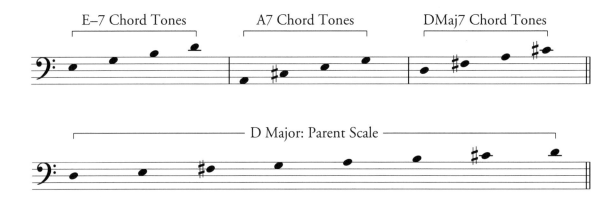

Now, let's continue examining the chord progression for chord tones. The next chord is D–7. This chord contains the note F, which is a departure from the previous region, where F was sharp in DMaj7. We are therefore beginning a new harmonic region, and D major will no longer be an effective source for our improvisation notes. Instead, the mode D Dorian can be derived from these chords, with C major as its parent scale.

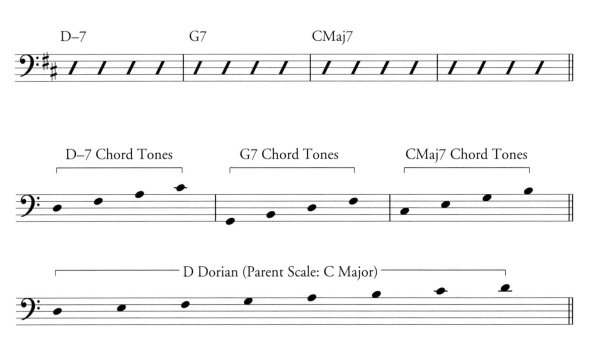

Continue this process, to see how long the chords remain within this new chord region. The next four chords all have notes in the mode of D Phrygian, with B♭ major as its parent scale.

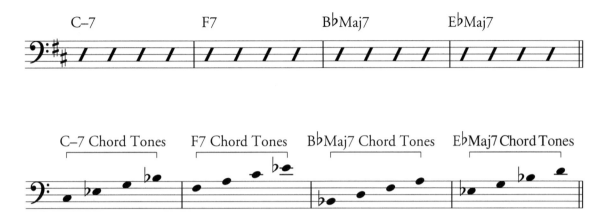

We will study the "Tune Up" progression in greater depth, later in this book.

Modes and Tetrachords

When you improvise, knowing the mode for each chord region gives you the tetrachords, and by practicing improvising using tetrachords, you will make your note choices more effective. Ultimately, you can build your ideas from either tetrachords or from the whole mode. You may decide this based on how comfortable you are with the music or your instrument, or the character you are trying to create in your soloing. Either approach will help you choose notes effectively.

For all these reasons, use of modes is one of the primary ways that we teach improvisation at Berklee. We will practice this approach in the next two lessons.

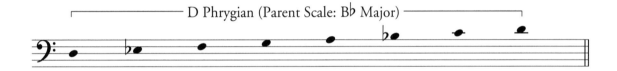

Lesson 4. Practice Vamp 1

Now, let's put pitch axes, tetrachords, and modes to work. This lesson and the next present short practice vamps that will help you understand this approach to improvisation. Then, the rest of the book will focus on using this approach in standard chord progressions.

The chord progression in this lesson can be improvised upon using the same mode all the way through. Remember, the root of the chord will not necessarily be the same as the root of the tetrachord.

GETTING ORIENTED

Listen to the chord progression to "Practice Vamp 1." Play and sing the chord roots along with the recording.

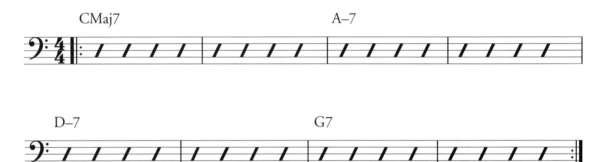

Bass Lines

Play this bass part along with the progression. Sing the roots as you play. What is this progression's pitch axis? What is the lower tetrachord? What is the upper tetrachord?

> Sing the note names of each chord root, as you play.

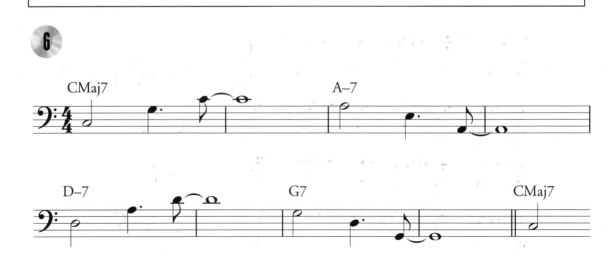

Practice Pads

Record a 30-second practice pad for each chord used in this progression: CMaj7, A–7, D–7, and G7.

This book's companion Web site at www.playingthechanges.com includes practice pads for all these chords, available for free download.

Analysis

The pitch axis for this progression is C. Its four chords (CMaj7, A–7, D–7, G7) all support the C major scale (Ionian mode) as their parent scale. Here, you can see which scale notes belong to each of the progression's chords.

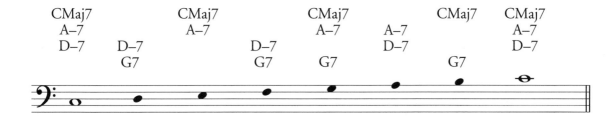

The lower tetrachord is C major.

The upper tetrachord is G major.

13

PRACTICE

Fingering

Warm up for improvising by practicing these tetrachord fingerings.

C Ionian

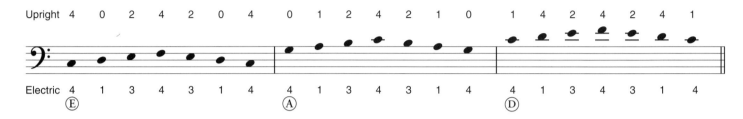

Pad Improvising

Record about thirty seconds of each chord in this progression: CMaj7, A–7, D–7, and G7. These will be your pads for practicing tetrachords.

Improvise over each chord pad, and concentrate on where the unstable notes resolve over each harmony. Play slowly, and listen for the relationship between the note you are playing and the harmony you are hearing. Hear the tension and resolution, and practice using it to create melodies—again, using only notes from the tetrachords.

Use the C major tetrachord and the G major tetrachord. Keep the tetrachords independent, but use both of them over every chord pad, repeating the tracks as necessary. Remember, when a tetrachord listed under the pitch tendencies is in bold type, there is a note in that tetrachord that requires special handling. Play it and listen for it.

PITCH TENDENCIES FOR PRACTICE PADS

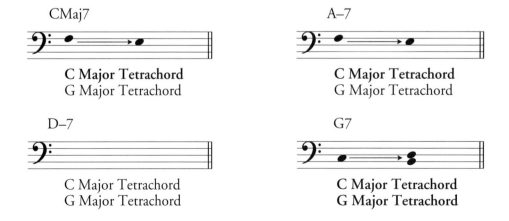

CMaj7

C Major Tetrachord
G Major Tetrachord

A–7

C Major Tetrachord
G Major Tetrachord

D–7

C Major Tetrachord
G Major Tetrachord

G7

C Major Tetrachord
G Major Tetrachord

Hearing Pitch Tendencies

When practicing these pitch tendencies, play notes of relatively long durations, so that you can hear the tension of the unstable notes. Play the unstable note. Then move to the stable note, and listen for how the stable note "relaxes" in relation to the chord. The strongest tendency of unstable notes is generally down a half step, but during improvisation, the melodic direction becomes more important.

Challenge

Record your own vamp using the chords from "Vamp 1" and your own bass-line ideas. Then practice improvising on your new vamp using the tetrachords. For an added challenge, practice singing your tetrachords while you play the bass line.

Finally, try practicing this progression in other keys. Write out the progression in another key, such as F. By following the steps in this lesson, come up with the mode and tetrachords to fit these new chords. Practice this progression, and listen for the tensions and resolutions.

Progression: Lower Tetrachord

This exercise and the next are like the pad exercise, except that the chords are played in time, with a rhythm section backing you up. Use the C major tetrachord to improvise over the chord progression. Listen for the following tendencies towards resolution, resolving from unstable notes to stable notes:

Chord	Resolution
CMaj7	F resolves down to E
A–7	F resolves down to E
G7	C resolves up to D

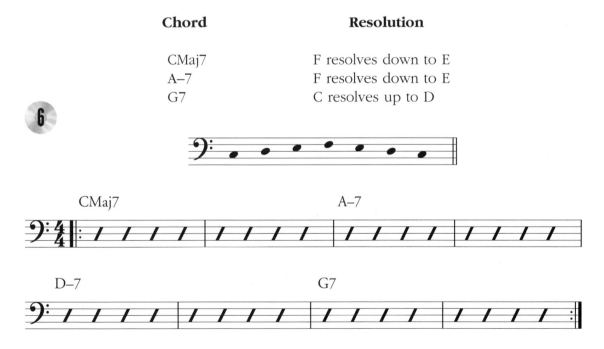

If you lose your place, just play roots for a few bars, until you regain your orientation.

Progression: Upper Tetrachord

Use the G major tetrachord to improvise over the chord progression. Listen for the following tendencies towards resolution:

Chord	Resolution
G7	C resolves down to B

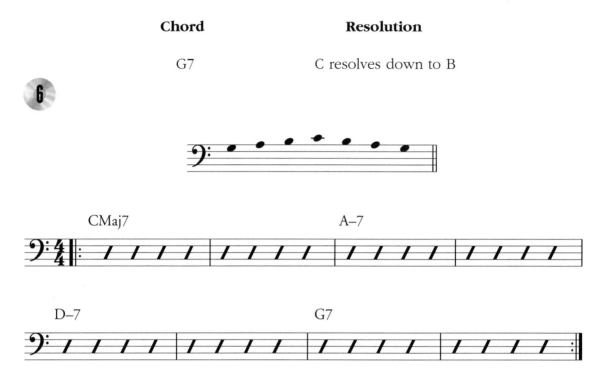

Progression: C Ionian Mode

Play the written half notes along with the recording. Listen to how each note fits each harmony. Consider what would be the natural resolving motion of each new note. Then continue the pattern, playing only half notes, up and down the scale, over the form.

Listen for the tension or sense of resolution of every note you play. When you continue, the next note you play should be E. You can also practice an expanded range by beginning this exercise on a different note of the mode, such as the low A. Later, we will expand this range.

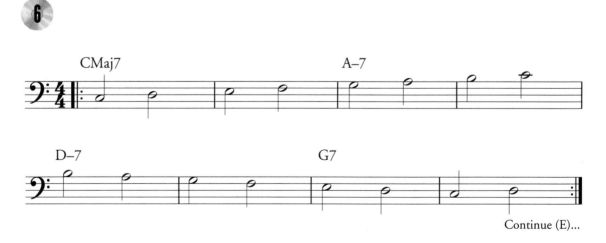

Continue (E)...

In that example, it took the vamp seven iterations to return to where it started. Next, begin the exercises on the note A instead, and extend the range up to a high G, using the fingering shown, or adjust the range to suit your technical ability on the bass.

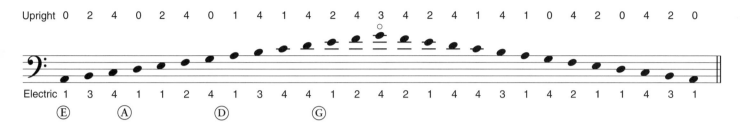

Keep repeating the pattern of half notes, going from A up to G, then back down to A, until you again play the note A against a CMaj7 chord.

Continue...

Mixed-Rhythm Modal Exercise

Finally, play this mixed-rhythm exercise. Again, listen to the sound of the notes against each chord. Continue cycling through the mode, using rhythm to control the stable and unstable notes.

The mixed-rhythm exercises are used to control or create a flow of the line. Longer durations are used with stable notes, and also to let the line rest or breathe. In all the mixed-rhythm mode exercises, analyze and listen carefully to where the line rests. This is fundamental to phrasing.

Continue...

Lesson 5. Practice Vamp 2: Two Modes

"Practice Vamp 2" can be improvised upon using two different modes.

GETTING ORIENTED

1 Listen to the progression. Play and sing the chord roots along with the recording.

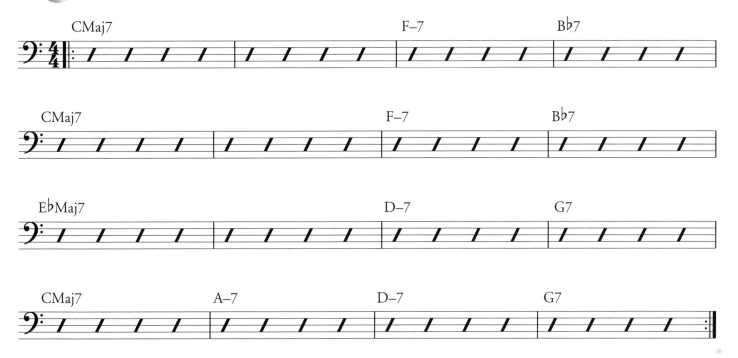

Bass Lines

1 Practice this bass line along with the progression. What is this progression's pitch axis?

Practice Pads

Record a 30-second practice pad for each chord used in this progression: CMaj7, F–7, Bb7, EbMaj7, D–7, G7, and A–7.

Analysis

The pitch axis for this progression is again C. Some of the chords are based on C major: CMaj7, G7, and A–7. Some of the chords are based on C minor: F–7, Bb7, and EbMaj7.

Mode 1. C Major (Ionian)

The lower tetrachord is C major.

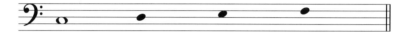

The upper tetrachord is G major.

Combined, these tetrachords form the C major scale (Ionian mode).

Mode 2. C Minor (Aeolian mode)

The lower tetrachord is C minor.

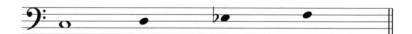

The upper tetrachord is G Phrygian.

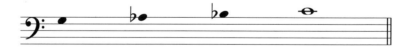

Combined, these tetrachords form the C minor scale (Aeolian mode).

PRACTICE

Fingering

Warm up for improvising by practicing these tetrachord fingerings.

C Ionian

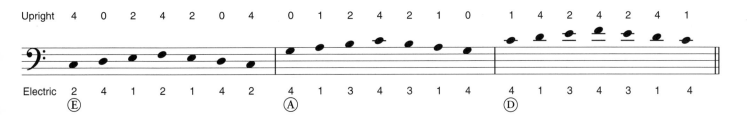

C Aeolian

Pad Improvising

Improvise over each chord pad. Practice the appropriate tetrachord over each chord, as shown. Keep the tetrachords intact, and repeat the exercise so that you can use both tetrachords over every harmony. Listen for where the unstable notes resolve, for each chord. (Tetrachords in bold include unstable notes that require special handling.)

1. Practice improvising in the lower tetrachord only. When you are ready to use the upper tetrachord, first play the root of the pad. Then move through the whole mode.

2. Practice improvising in the upper tetrachord only. When you are ready to use the whole mode, first play the root of the pad.

3. Practice improvising while moving throughout the entire mode. End the exercise on the root of the pad.

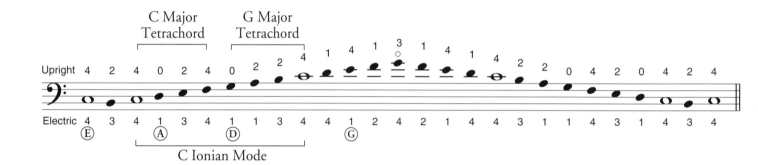

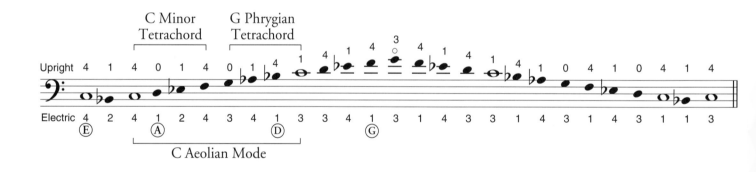

PITCH TENDENCIES FOR PRACTICE PADS

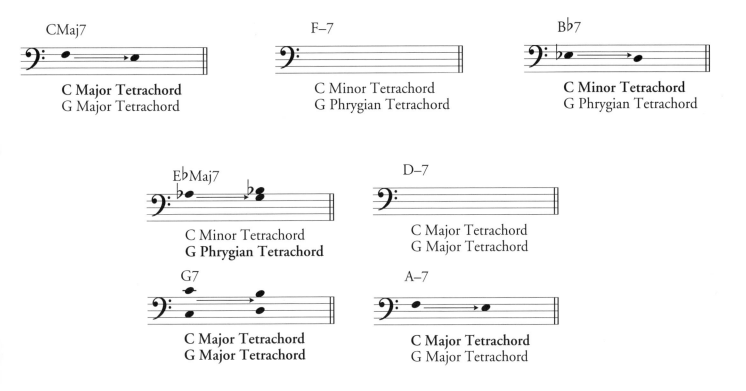

C Major Tetrachord
G Major Tetrachord

C Minor Tetrachord
G Phrygian Tetrachord

C Minor Tetrachord
G Phrygian Tetrachord

C Minor Tetrachord
G Phrygian Tetrachord

C Major Tetrachord
G Major Tetrachord

C Major Tetrachord
G Major Tetrachord

C Major Tetrachord
G Major Tetrachord

Record Your Own

Record your own pads using these chords. Then practice improvising on your new pads using the tetrachords. For an added challenge, burn your pads onto a CD and use the "shuffle" feature to change pads randomly. Or best of all, have a friend play pads while you practice improvising. Then switch roles. There are many ways to practice by using chord pads.

Tetrachord Practice: C Major and C Minor

Use the C major and C minor tetrachords to improvise over the vamp. Practice in all octaves. Then try this exercise while reading the chord chart at the beginning of this lesson, without the tetrachords labeled. Listen for the following tendencies towards resolution:

Chord	Resolution
CMaj7	F moves down to E
B♭7	E♭ moves down to D
G7	C moves up to D
A–7	F moves down to E

C Major Tetrachord

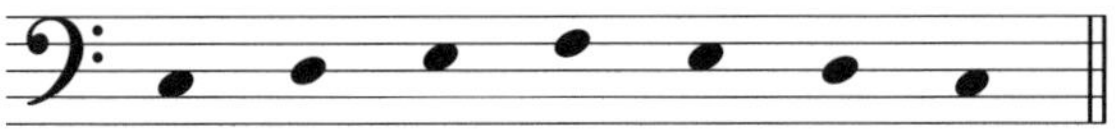

C Minor Tetrachord

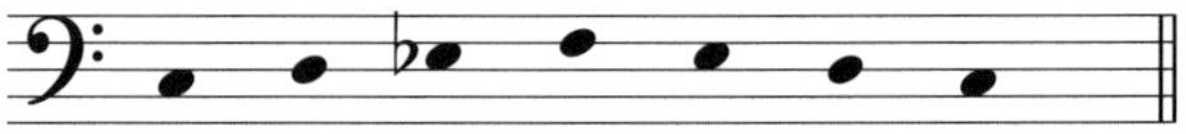

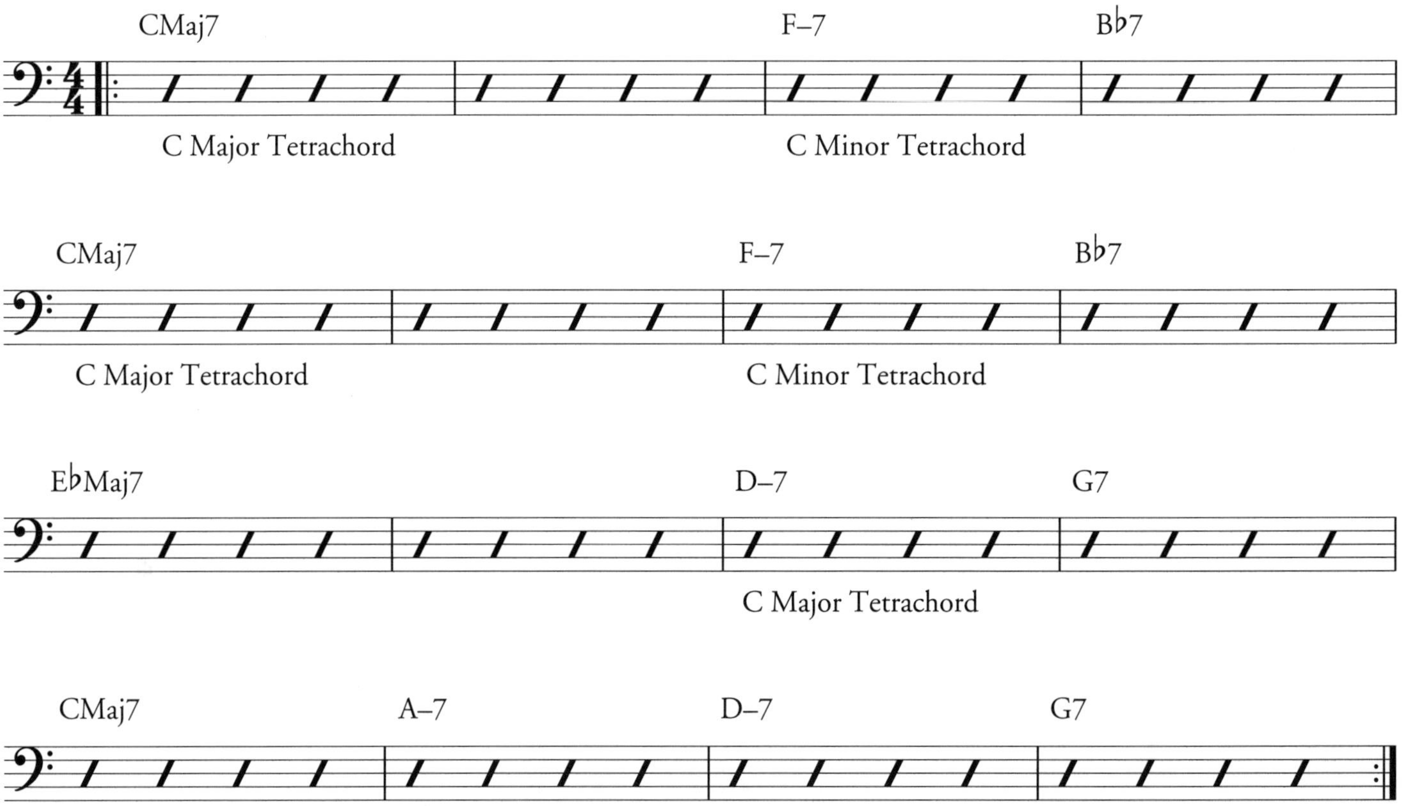

Tetrachord Practice: G Major and G Phrygian

Use the G major and G Phrygian tetrachords to improvise over the progression. Listen for the following tendencies towards resolution:

Chord	Resolution
E♭Maj7	A♭ moves down to G or up to B♭
G7	C moves down to B

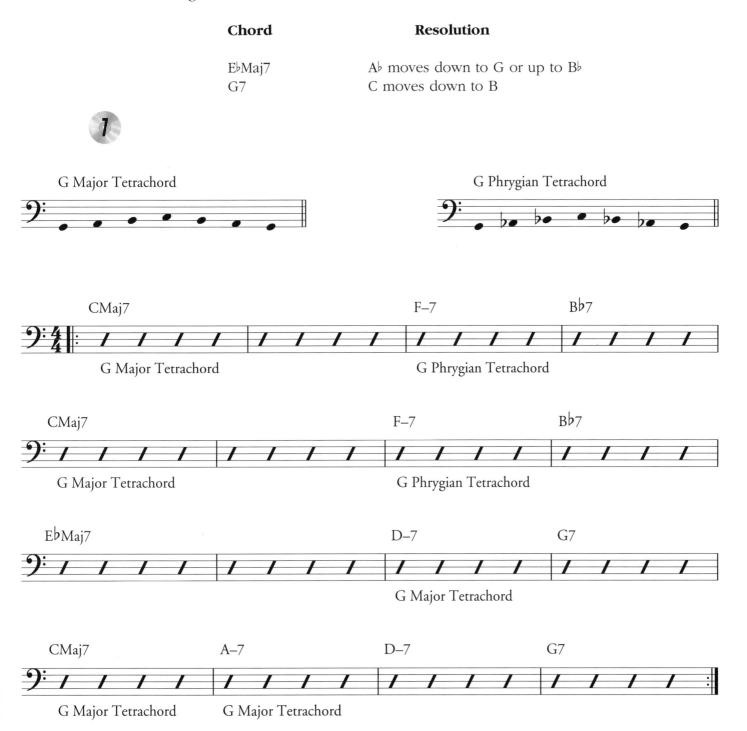

Mode Practice

Play the written half notes along with the recording. Listen to how each note fits each harmony, and notice how the notes change to fit the mode of each harmony. Then continue the pattern, playing only half notes, up and down the scale, over the form, and be sure to choose the correct half note for each harmony you encounter.

This exercise is at the heart of this method, and it is a powerful tool to help you choose notes to go with harmonies. All rhythms are half notes, and the line simply goes up and down the range. Your focused task is to choose the note from the proper scale to fit over each harmony. This isolates the decision process you must go through. It is a very focused form of improvisation, and will help you develop your expectation of sound.

Linking Modes

At the first beat of bar 3, we switch modes. The link between the two modes is the D moving to the E♭.

Continue...

Changing Tone vs. Common Tone

If the mode is changing and you are about to move a whole step, first consider whether there is a half step available instead.

Mixed-Rhythm Modal Exercise

Finally, play this mixed-rhythm exercise. Again, listen to the sound of the notes against each chord. Continue cycling through the mode, and use rhythm to control the stable and unstable notes.

Continue...

Write It Out

If you need to, write out the continuation of this exercise for a chorus. But work to be able to play it by ear, spontaneously.

27

PART II. Progressions

Now, we will use these tools in standard chord progressions. Each of the following lessons is based on a chord progression from the "standard" jazz repertoire. Many songs (or sections of songs) have been written based on each of these progressions.

When you become comfortable playing these standards, learning many new tunes will become much easier.

As you saw in the Practice Vamp lessons, you will learn the chord progression from several perspectives. First, you'll listen to it and analyze it to find its pitch axis. Next, you will practice a bass line and create practice pads. Then you will practice the tetrachords in different registers, learning some fingering tips, and improvise on each chord of the progression in isolation, listening for each tetrachord note's pitch tendencies, when played against each chord.

At that point, you will be well prepared to solo over the progression, linearly. You'll start with one tetrachord, then the other, and finally the entire mode, practicing the process of determining and hearing when the mode changes for a given harmony.

You'll have the opportunity to read and hear my sample solo for the progression. And then finally, you will be free to improvise your own solo and practice improvising new solos on the spot.

Through all these ways of approaching the chord progression, you will master it completely. When you come across another tune that includes this progression, perhaps in another key or groove, you will learn it much more easily, since you will already be familiar with its sound.

Lesson 6. Two Modes

This progression is based on the changes to "Blue Bossa," by Kenny Dorham.

GETTING ORIENTED

Listen to this chord progression. Play and sing the chord roots along with the recording.

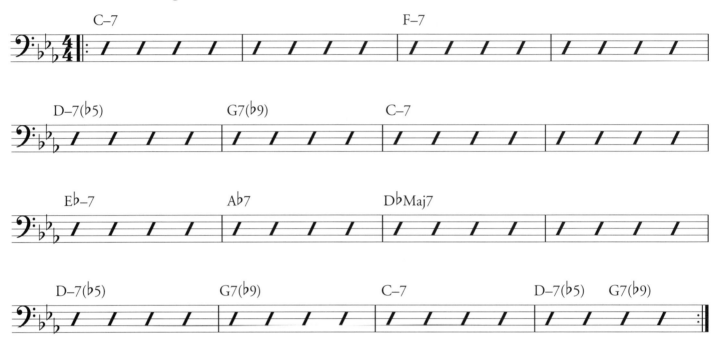

Bass Lines

Practice this bass part along with the progression. Sing the roots as you play. What is this progression's pitch axis (see lesson 1)?

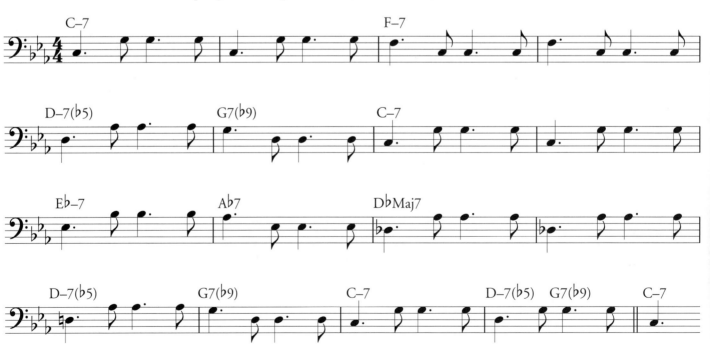

Practice Pads

Record a 30-second practice pad for each chord used in this progression: C–7, F–7, D–7(♭5), G7(♭9), E♭–7, A♭7, and D♭Maj7.

Analysis

Using the analysis approach discussed earlier, we can determine that the pitch axis for this progression is again C. (We will be exploring new pitch axes in the coming lessons.) Some of the chords are based on C Aeolian; some are based on C Locrian.

Mode 1. C Aeolian

The lower tetrachord is C minor (C–7, F7, D–7[♭5], G7[♭9]). The upper tetrachord is G Phrygian (C–7, F7, D–7[♭5], G7[♭9]). Combined, these tetrachords form the C Aeolian mode.

B♭ vs. B♮ over G7(♭9)

When you improvise over this G7(♭9) chord, try using the B♭ (from C Phrygian), rather than the B♮ (from the chord). Though the B♮ is a chord tone, using the B♭ is a more linear approach to improvisation, and it will be more melodically effective. The B♮ will suit the harmony, but will not have the same forward momentum, as it will be more detached from its surrounding notes in the melody.

Mode 2. C Locrian

The lower tetrachord is C Phrygian (E♭–7, A♭7, D♭Maj7). The upper tetrachord is G♭ Lydian (E♭–7, A♭7, D♭Maj7). Combined, these tetrachords form the C Locrian mode.

PRACTICE

Fingering

Warm up for improvising by practicing these tetrachord fingerings. Note that electric bass fingerings for tetrachords involve no shifts.

C Aeolian

C Locrian

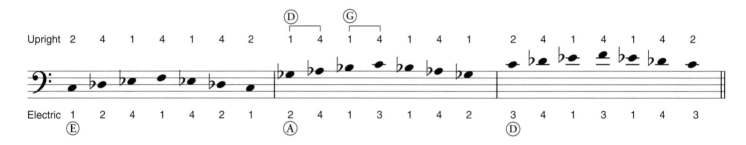

Sing with Your Instrument

As you practice, sing with your instrument. Listen to the quality of each tetrachord. Play slowly enough to hear and think about the intervals in each one.

Pad Improvising

Improvise over your recorded chord pads, singing each note as you play. Practice the appropriate mode's tetrachords over each chord, as shown. Use just one tetrachord at a time, and repeat the pads so that you can use both tetrachords of the given mode. Listen for where the unstable notes resolve, for each chord. (Tetrachords in **bold** include notes that require special handling.) Note that in D♭Maj7, when using the whole mode, the G♭ will tend to resolve down to F.

Follow these steps for each pad:

1. Practice improvising in the lower tetrachord only. When you are ready to use the upper tetrachord, first play the note G or G♭, depending on the pad.

2. Practice improvising in the upper tetrachord only. When you are ready to use the whole mode, first play the root of the pad.

3. Practice improvising while moving throughout the entire mode. End the exercise on the root of the pad.

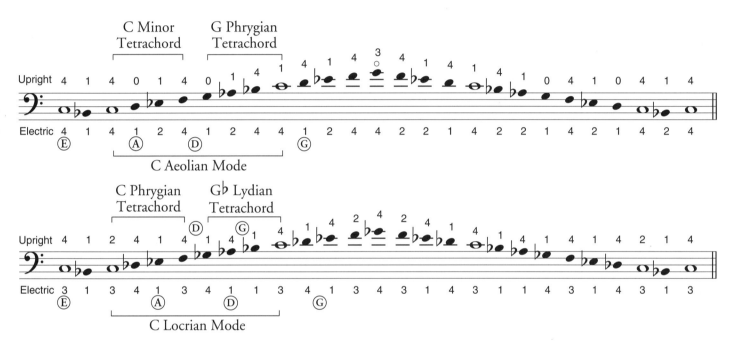

PITCH TENDENCIES FOR PRACTICE PADS

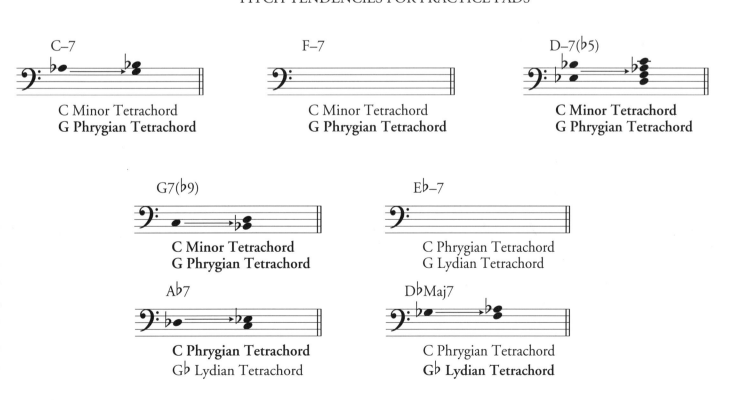

Tetrachord Practice

Improvise over the chord progression, using the appropriate tetrachord over each chord. Practice using each tetrachord in all octaves. Then try this exercise while reading the chord progression at the beginning of this lesson, without the tetrachords labeled.

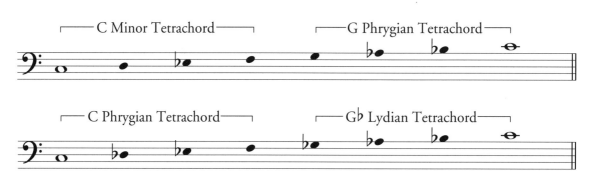

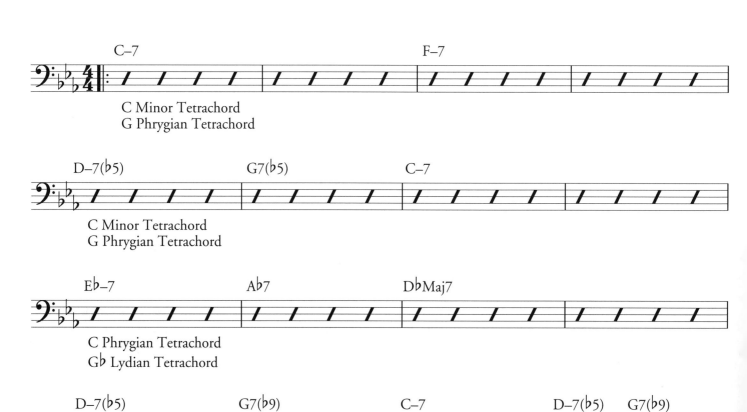

Mode Practice

Play the written half notes along with the recording, listening for how the unstable notes resolve to stable notes. Continue the pattern, choosing the correct half note for each harmony you encounter.

Continue...

Mixed-Rhythm Modal Exercise

Next, play this mixed-rhythm exercise. Again, listen to the sound of the notes against each chord. Continue cycling through the modes, and use rhythm to control stable and unstable notes.

Linking Modes

Remember to look for the half step as the mode changes. In bar 9, at the Eb–7 chord, play a Db, rather than a C. By moving to the closest possible note in the new mode (in this case, a half step), you'll make a smoother transition. Think of this as the link between the two modes.

PERFORMANCE

Etude

Practice this etude along with track 8 on the recording, singing it as you play. Analyze its use of tetrachords and modes, and notice how the unstable notes resolve. It is demonstrated on track 9.

> You may prefer to begin practicing this solo in unison with the recorded line, on track 9—particularly if you have difficulty in reading. Once you have learned it, practice it with track 8.

Solo

1. Improvise a solo over the "Blue Bossa" changes. When you're comfortable with this progression, record your solo.

2. Transcribe the best two choruses of your improvised solo, and rewrite them as you see fit.

3. Practice playing this final solo along with the recording, using it to lead into further improvisations.

Challenge

Transpose this progression to another key, such as A minor. Then use the process outlined in this method to improvise a solo over it. Notice how much more easily you can learn the new progression, since the essential progression is already known to you.

Lesson 7. Three Modes

This progression is based on the changes to "Tune Up," by Miles Davis. (Some claim it was Eddie "Cleanhead" Vinson, but most credit Miles Davis.)

GETTING ORIENTED

Listen to this chord progression. Play and sing the chord roots along with the recording.

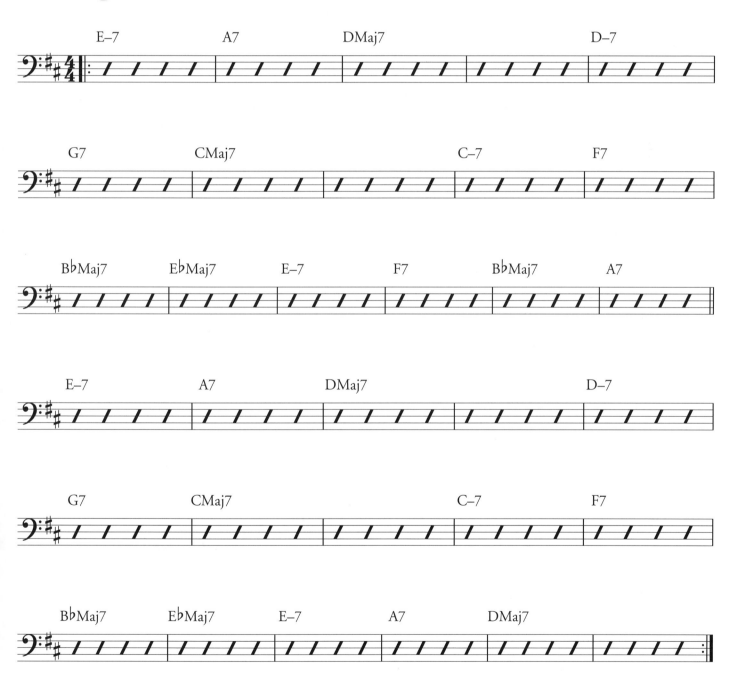

Bass Lines

Practice this bass part along with the progression. What is this progression's pitch axis?

Practice Pads

Record a 30-second practice pad for each chord used in this progression: E–7, A7, DMaj7, D–7, G7, CMaj7, C–7, F7, B♭Maj7, and E♭Maj7.

Analysis

The pitch axis for this progression is D. The chords yield three modes (D Ionian, D Dorian, and D Phrygian), which are built from six tetrachords (D major, D minor, D Phrygian, A major, A minor, and A Phrygian).

Mode 1. D Ionian

The lower tetrachord is D major (E–7, A7, DMaj7). The upper tetrachord is A major (E–7, A7, DMaj7). Combined, these tetrachords form the D Ionian mode.

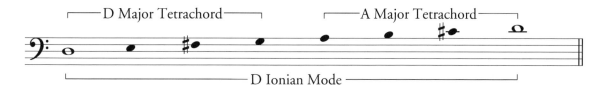

Mode 2. D Dorian

The lower tetrachord is D minor (D–7, G7, CMaj7). The upper tetrachord is A minor (D–7, G7, CMaj7). Combined, these tetrachords form the D Dorian mode.

Mode 3. D Phrygian

The lower tetrachord is D Phrygian (C–7, F7, B♭Maj7, E♭Maj7). The upper tetrachord is A Phrygian (C–7, F7, B♭Maj7, E♭Maj7). Combined, these tetrachords form the D Phrygian mode.

PRACTICE

Fingering

Warm up for improvising by practicing these tetrachord fingerings.

D Ionian

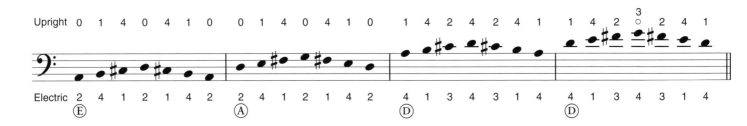

D Dorian

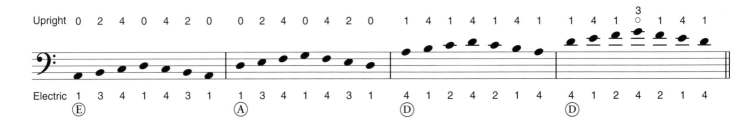

D Phrygian

Pad Improvising

Improvise over each of your recorded chord pads. Practice the appropriate mode's tetrachords over each chord, as shown. Use just one tetrachord at a time, and repeat the pads so that you can use both tetrachords of the given mode. Listen for where the unstable notes resolve, for each chord. (Tetrachords in **bold** include notes that require special handling.)

Follow these steps for each pad:

1. Practice improvising in the lower tetrachord only. When you are ready to use the upper tetrachord, first play the note A.

2. Practice improvising in the upper tetrachord only. When you are ready to use the whole mode, first play the root of the pad.

3. Practice improvising while moving throughout the entire mode. End the exercise on the root of the pad.

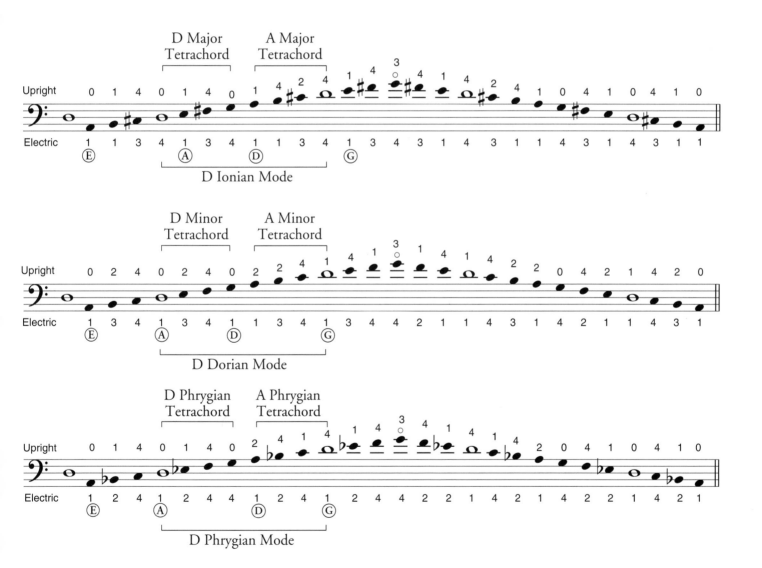

PITCH TENDENCIES FOR PRACTICE PADS

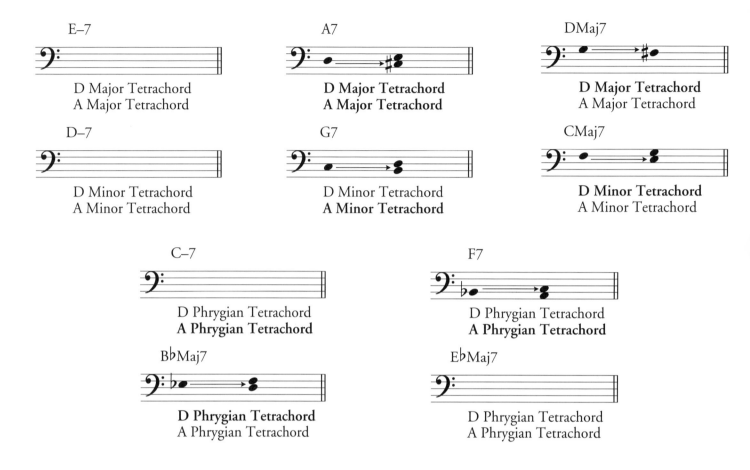

Tetrachord Practice

Improvise over the chord progression, using the appropriate tetrachord over each chord. Practice using each tetrachord in all octaves. Then try this exercise while reading the chord progression at the beginning of this lesson, without the tetrachords labeled.

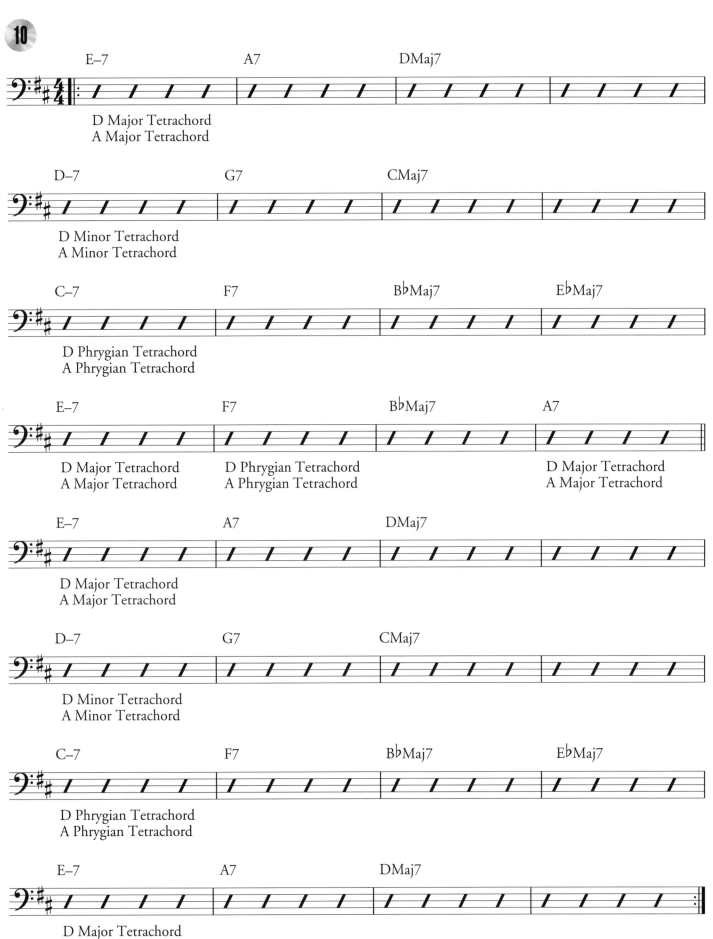

Mode Practice

Play the written half notes along with the recording. Continue the pattern, choosing the correct half note for each harmony you encounter. Notice how the linking points between modes are always the closest possible interval.

Continue...

Key Signatures

Be careful of the key signature in this example.

Mixed-Rhythm Modal Exercise

Next, play this mixed-rhythm exercise. Again, listen to the sound of the notes against each chord. Continue cycling through the modes, and use rhythm to control stable and unstable notes.

Continue...

PERFORMANCE

Etude

Practice this etude along with the recording, track 10, singing it as you play. Analyze its use of tetrachords and modes, and notice how the unstable notes resolve. It is demonstrated on track 11.

Solo

1. Improvise a solo over the "Tune Up" changes. When you're comfortable with this progression, record your solo.

2. Transcribe the best chorus of your improvised solo, and rewrite it as you see fit.

3. Practice playing this final solo along with the recording, using it to lead into further improvisations.

Lesson 8. Three Modes

This progression is based on the changes to "Valse Hot," by Sonny Rollins.

GETTING ORIENTED

12 Listen to the chord progression. Play and sing the chord roots along with the recording.

Bass Lines

12 Practice this bass part along with the progression. Sing the roots as you play. What is this progression's pitch axis?

Practice Pads

Record a 30-second practice pad for each chord used in this progression: A♭Maj7, C–7, F7(♭9), B♭–7, E♭7, and D♭–7.

Analysis

The pitch axis for this progression is A♭. The chords yield three modes (A♭ Ionian, A♭ Mixolydian, and A♭ Aeolian), which are built from five tetrachords (A♭ major, A♭ minor, E♭ major, E♭ minor, E♭ Phrygian).

Mode 1. A♭ Ionian

The lower tetrachord is A♭ major (A♭Maj7, B♭–7, C–7, E♭7, F7[♭9]). The upper tetrachord is E♭ major (A♭Maj7, B♭–7, C–7, E♭7). Combined, these tetrachords form the A♭ Ionian mode.

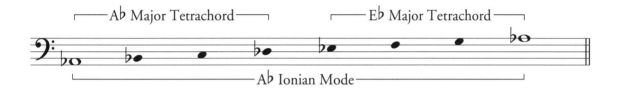

Mode 2. A♭ Mixolydian

The lower tetrachord is A♭ major (A♭Maj7, B♭–7, C–7, E♭7, F7[♭9]). The upper tetrachord is E♭ minor (F7[♭9]). Combined, these tetrachords form the A♭ Mixolydian mode.

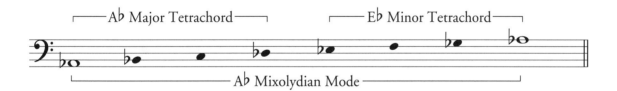

Mode 3. A♭ Aeolian

The lower tetrachord is A♭ minor (D♭–7). The upper tetrachord is E♭ Phrygian (D♭–7). Combined, these tetrachords form the A♭ Aeolian mode.

PRACTICE

Fingering

Warm up for improvising by practicing these tetrachord fingerings.

A♭ Ionian

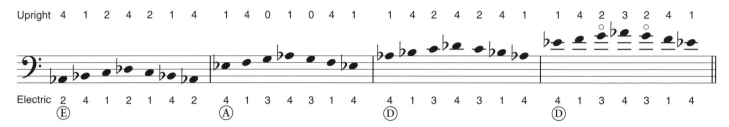

A♭ Mixolydian

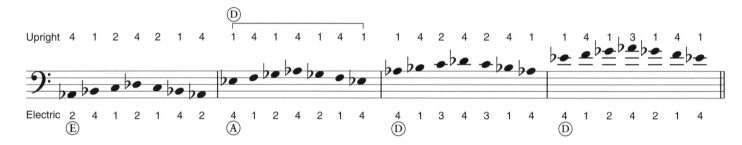

A♭ Aeolian

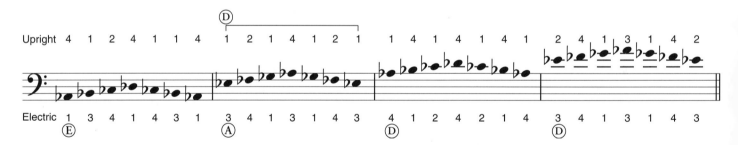

Pad Improvising

Improvise over each of your recorded chord pads. Practice the appropriate mode's tetrachords over each chord, as shown. Use just one tetrachord at a time, and repeat the pads so that you can use both tetrachords of the given mode. Listen for where the unstable notes resolve, for each chord. (Tetrachords in **bold** include notes that require special handling.)

Follow these steps for each pad:

1. Practice improvising in the lower tetrachord only. When you are ready to use the upper tetrachord, first play the note E♭.

2. Practice improvising in the upper tetrachord only. When you are ready to use the whole mode, first play the root of the pad.

3. Practice improvising while moving throughout the entire mode. End the exercise on the root of the pad.

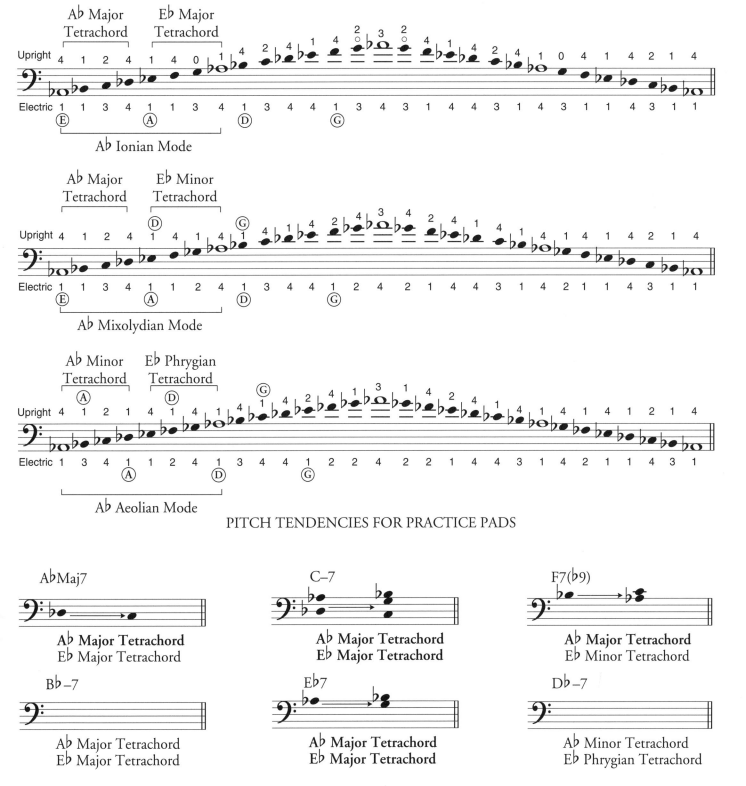

PITCH TENDENCIES FOR PRACTICE PADS

> **Note: The A♭ in F7(♭9)**
>
> In F7(♭9), even though the A is included in the chord, use the A♭ instead. It has a more distinguishable sound. Listen for that quality as you practice this chord pad.

Tetrachord Practice

Improvise over the chord progression, using the appropriate tetrachord over each chord. Practice using each tetrachord in all octaves. Then try this exercise while reading the chord progression at the beginning of this lesson, without the tetrachords labeled.

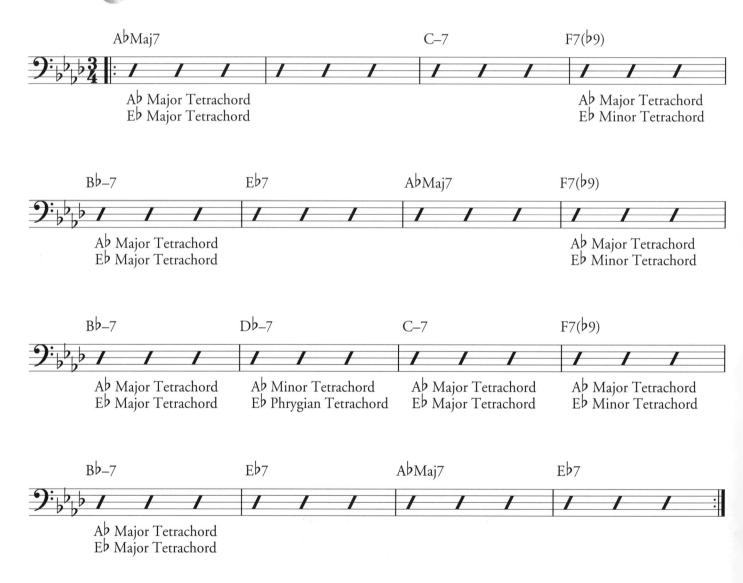

Mode Practice

Play the written notes along with the recording. Continue the pattern, choosing the correct note for each harmony you encounter. This exercise can also be played with the following rhythm: | $\frac{3}{4}$ ♩. ♩. |, or with combinations of both rhythms.

Continue...

Mixed-Rhythm Modal Exercise

Next, play this mixed-rhythm exercise. Again, listen to the sound of the notes against
each chord. Continue cycling through the modes, and use rhythm to control stable and
unstable notes.

Continue...

PERFORMANCE

Etude

Practice this etude along with the recording, track 12, singing it as you play. Analyze its use of tetrachords and modes, and notice how the unstable notes resolve. It is demonstrated on track 13.

Solo

1. Improvise a solo over the "Valse Hot" changes. When you're comfortable with this progression, record your solo.

2. Transcribe the best two choruses of your improvised solo, and rewrite them as you see fit.

3. Practice playing this final solo along with the recording, using it to lead into further improvisations.

Lesson 9. Three Modes

This lesson is based on a standard 12-bar blues progression.

GETTING ORIENTED

14 Listen to this blues chord progression. Play and sing the chord roots along with the recording.

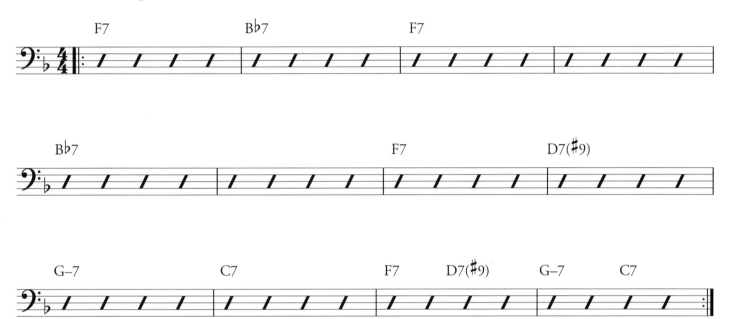

Bass Lines

14 Practice this bass part along with the progression. What is this progression's pitch axis?

Practice Pads

Record a 30-second practice pad for each chord used in this progression: F7, B♭7, D7(♯9), G–7, and C7.

Analysis

The pitch axis for this progression is F. The chords yield three modes (F Mixolydian, F Dorian, and F Ionian), which are built from four tetrachords (F major, F minor, C major, and C minor).

Mode 1. F Mixolydian

The lower tetrachord is F major (F7, G–7, C7, D7[♯9]). The upper tetrachord is C minor (F7, B♭7, D7[♯9]). Combined, these tetrachords form the F Mixolydian mode.

Mode 2. F Dorian

The lower tetrachord is F minor (B♭7). The upper tetrachord is C minor (F7, B♭7, D7[♯9]). Combined, these tetrachords form the F Dorian mode.

Mode 3. F Ionian

The lower tetrachord is F major (F7, G–7, C7, D7[♯9]). The upper tetrachord is C major (G–7, C7). Combined, these tetrachords form the F Ionian mode.

PRACTICE

Fingering

Warm up for improvising by practicing these tetrachord fingerings.

F Mixolydian

F Dorian

F Ionian

Pad Improvising

Improvise over each of your recorded chord pads. Practice the appropriate mode's tetrachords over each chord, as shown. Use just one tetrachord at a time, and repeat the pads so that you can use both tetrachords of the given mode. Listen for where the unstable notes resolve, for each chord. (Tetrachords in **bold** include notes that require special handling.)

Follow these steps for each pad:

1. Practice improvising in the lower tetrachord only. When you are ready to use the upper tetrachord, first play the note C.

2. Practice improvising in the upper tetrachord only. When you are ready to use the whole mode, first play the root of the pad.

3. Practice improvising while moving throughout the entire mode. End the exercise on the root of the pad.

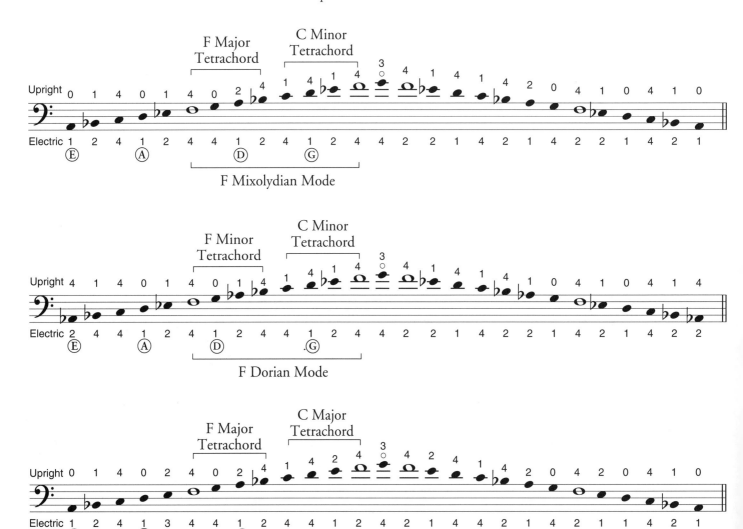

PITCH TENDENCIES FOR PRACTICE PADS

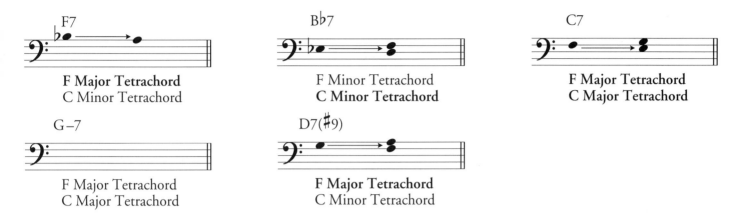

F7

F Major Tetrachord
C Minor Tetrachord

Bb7

F Minor Tetrachord
C Minor Tetrachord

C7

F Major Tetrachord
C Major Tetrachord

G–7

F Major Tetrachord
C Major Tetrachord

D7(♯9)

F Major Tetrachord
C Minor Tetrachord

F♯ vs. F♮ over D7(♯9)

In D7(♯9), even though the F♯ is included in the chord, use the F♮ instead. It has a more distinguishable sound. Listen for that quality, as you practice this chord pad.

Tetrachord Practice

Improvise over the chord progression, using the appropriate tetrachord over each chord. Practice using each tetrachord in all octaves. Then try this exercise while reading the chord progression at the beginning of this lesson, without the tetrachords labeled.

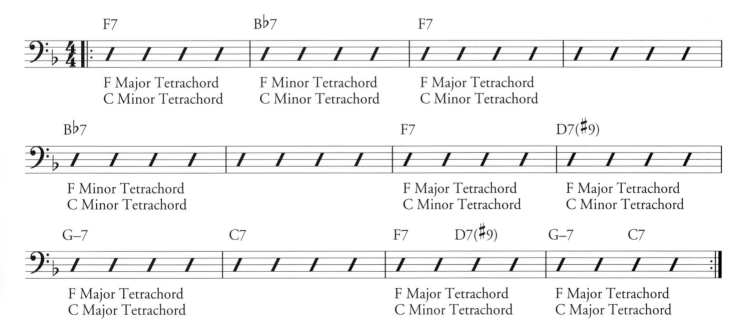

F7

F Major Tetrachord
C Minor Tetrachord

Bb7

F Minor Tetrachord
C Minor Tetrachord

F7

F Major Tetrachord
C Minor Tetrachord

Bb7

F Minor Tetrachord
C Minor Tetrachord

F7

F Major Tetrachord
C Minor Tetrachord

D7(♯9)

F Major Tetrachord
C Minor Tetrachord

G–7

F Major Tetrachord
C Major Tetrachord

C7

F7   D7(♯9)

F Major Tetrachord
C Minor Tetrachord

G–7   C7

F Major Tetrachord
C Major Tetrachord

Mode Practice

Play the written half notes along with the recording. Continue the pattern, choosing the correct half note for each harmony you encounter.

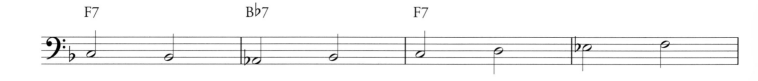

Continue...

Mixed-Rhythm Modal Exercise

Next, play this mixed-rhythm exercise. Again, listen to the sound of the notes against each chord. Continue cycling through the modes, and use rhythm to control stable and unstable notes.

Continue...

PERFORMANCE

Etude

Practice this etude along with the recording, track 14, singing it as you play. Analyze its use of tetrachords and modes, and notice how the unstable notes resolve. It is demonstrated on track 15.

Solo

1. Improvise a solo over these blues changes. When you're comfortable with this progression, record your solo.

2. Transcribe the best two choruses of your improvised solo, and rewrite them as you see fit.

3. Practice playing this final solo along with the recording, using it to lead into further improvisations.

Lesson 10. Four Modes

This progression is based on the changes to "Long Ago and Far Away," by Jerome Kern (lyrics by Ira Gershwin).

GETTING ORIENTED

Listen to the chord progression. Play and sing the chord roots along with the recording.

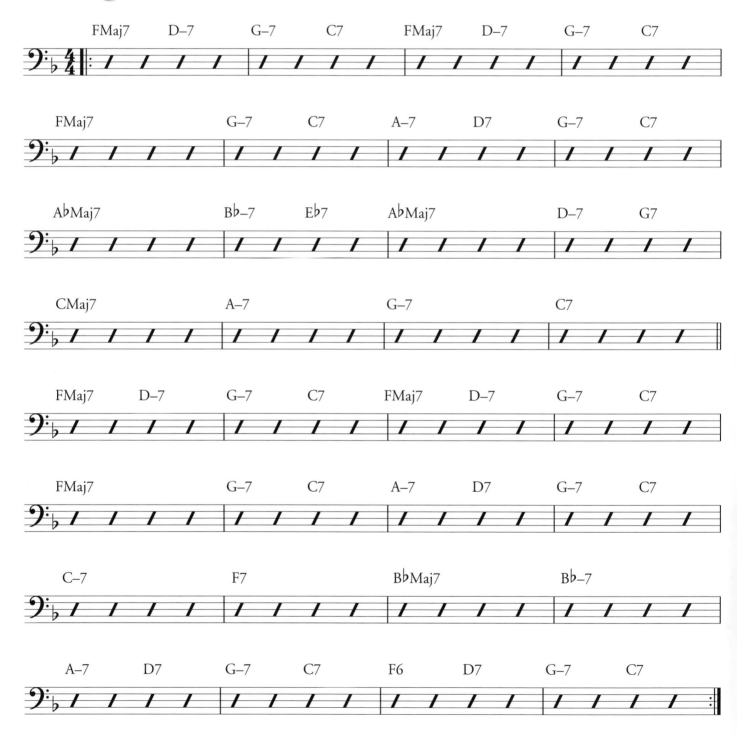

Bass Lines

Practice this bass part along with the progression. Sing the roots as you play. What is this progression's pitch axis?

Practice Pads

Record a 30-second practice pad for each chord used in this progression: FMaj7, D–7, G–7, C7, A–7, D7, A♭Maj7, B♭–7, E♭7, G7, CMaj7, A–7, C–7, F7, B♭Maj7, and F6.

Analysis

The pitch axis for this progression is F. The chords yield four modes (F Ionian, F Mixolydian, F Aeolian, and F Lydian), which are built from six tetrachords (F major, F minor, F Lydian, C major, C minor, and C Phrygian).

Mode 1. F Ionian

The lower tetrachord is F major (FMaj, D–7, G–7, C7, C–7, F7, B♭Maj7, A–7, D7*, F6). The upper tetrachord is C major (FMaj7, D–7, G–7, C7, G7, F6). Combined, these tetrachords form the F Ionian mode.

---

*Why F Ionian for D7?

If the chord tones for D7 are D, F♯, A, and C, why use the F Ionian mode, since it is based on F♮, rather than F♯? There are two primary reasons.

1. The D7 chord is functioning within the progression's overall key, which is strongly in F major.

2. The D7 chord's duration is very short, and a switch to a mode with F♯ would be cumbersome and distracting, and disruptive to the linear effect.

Mode 2. F Mixolydian

The lower tetrachord is F major (FMaj7, D–7, G–7, C7, C–7, F7, B♭Maj7, D7, F6). The upper tetrachord is C minor (C–7, F7, B♭Maj7). Combined, these tetrachords form the F Mixolydian mode.

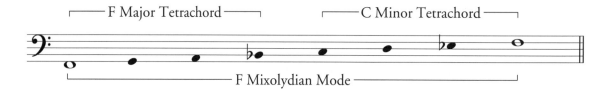

Mode 3. F Aeolian

The lower tetrachord is F minor (A♭Maj7, B♭–7, E♭7). The upper tetrachord is C Phrygian (A♭Maj7, B♭–7, E♭7). Combined, these tetrachords form the F Aeolian mode.

Mode 4. F Lydian

The lower tetrachord is F Lydian (CMaj7, D–7, G7). The upper tetrachord is C major (FMaj7, D–7, G–7, C7, A–7, CMaj7, F6). Combined, these tetrachords form the F Lydian mode.

PRACTICE

Fingering

Warm up for improvising by practicing these tetrachord fingerings.

F Ionian

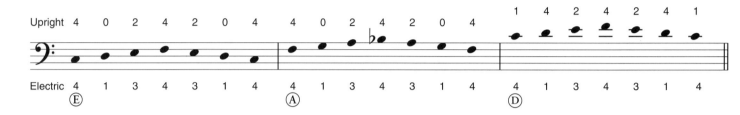

F Mixolydian

F Aeolian

F Lydian

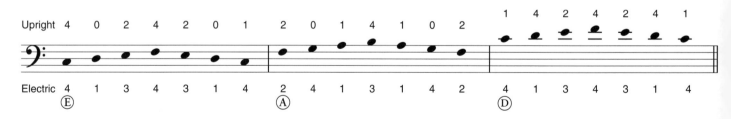

Pad Improvising

Improvise over each of your recorded chord pads. Practice the appropriate mode's tetrachords over each chord, as shown. Use just one tetrachord at a time, and repeat the pads so that you can use both tetrachords of the given mode. Listen for where the unstable notes resolve, for each chord. (Tetrachords in **bold** include notes that require special handling.)

Follow these steps for each pad:

1. Practice improvising in the lower tetrachord only. When you are ready to use the upper tetrachord, first play the note C.

2. Practice improvising in the upper tetrachord only. When you are ready to use the whole mode, first play the root of the pad.

3. Practice improvising while moving throughout the entire mode. End the exercise on the root of the pad.

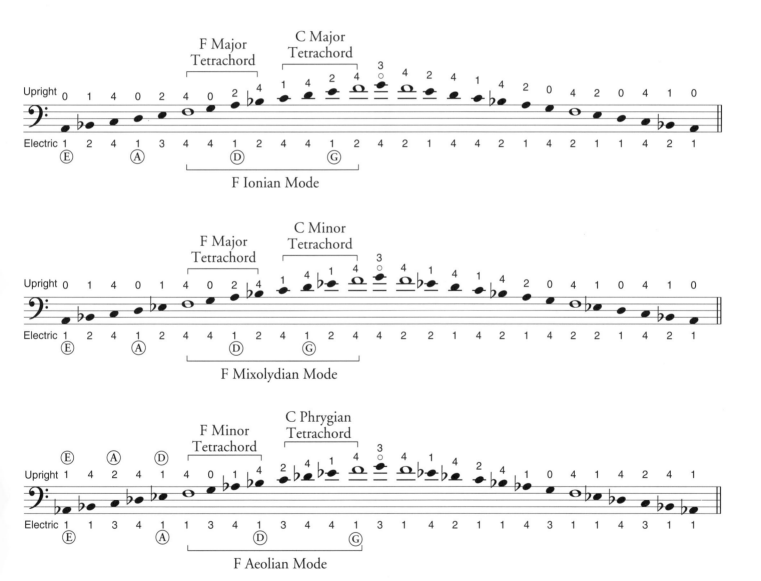

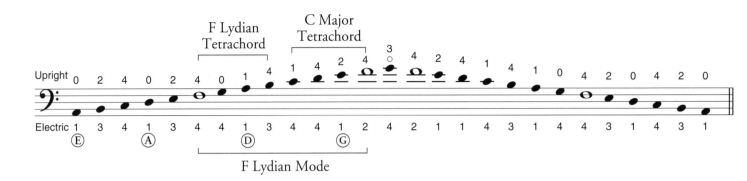

PITCH TENDENCIES FOR PRACTICE PADS

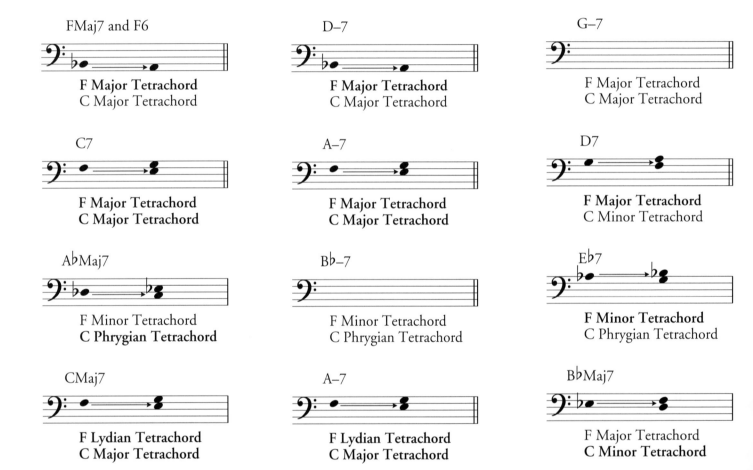

FMaj7 and F6
F Major Tetrachord
C Major Tetrachord

D–7
F Major Tetrachord
C Major Tetrachord

G–7
F Major Tetrachord
C Major Tetrachord

C7
F Major Tetrachord
C Major Tetrachord

A–7
F Major Tetrachord
C Major Tetrachord

D7
F Major Tetrachord
C Minor Tetrachord

A♭Maj7
F Minor Tetrachord
C Phrygian Tetrachord

B♭–7
F Minor Tetrachord
C Phrygian Tetrachord

E♭7
F Minor Tetrachord
C Phrygian Tetrachord

CMaj7
F Lydian Tetrachord
C Major Tetrachord

A–7
F Lydian Tetrachord
C Major Tetrachord

B♭Maj7
F Major Tetrachord
C Minor Tetrachord

Tetrachord Practice

Improvise over the chord progression, using the appropriate tetrachord over each chord. Practice using each tetrachord in all octaves. Then try this exercise while reading the chord progression at the beginning of this lesson, without the tetrachords labeled.

Mode Practice

Play the written half notes along with the recording. Continue the pattern, choosing the correct half note for each harmony you encounter.

Continue...

Mixed-Rhythm Modal Exercise

Next, play this mixed-rhythm exercise. Again, listen to the sound of the notes against each chord. Continue cycling through the modes, and use rhythm to control stable and unstable notes. Notice the use of quarter-note triplets.

Continue...

PERFORMANCE

Etude

Practice this etude along with the recording, track 16, singing it as you play. Analyze its use of tetrachords and modes, and notice how the unstable notes resolve. Also notice its use of quarter-note triplets. It is demonstrated on track 17.

Solo

1. Improvise a solo over the "Long Ago and Far Away" changes. When you're comfortable with this progression, record your solo.

2. Transcribe the best chorus of your improvised solo, and rewrite it as you see fit.

3. Practice playing this final solo along with the recording, using it to lead into further improvisations.

Lesson 11. Four Modes

This lesson is based on the progression used in "Lady Bird" by Tadd Dameron and Stanley Cornfield, "Half Nelson" by Nelson Boyd, and other tunes. The chords in the last two bars are like the beginning of "Here's That Rainy Day" by Jimmy Van Heusen. It's also a common turnaround progression in jazz.

GETTING ORIENTED

Listen to this progression. Play and sing the chord roots along with the recording.

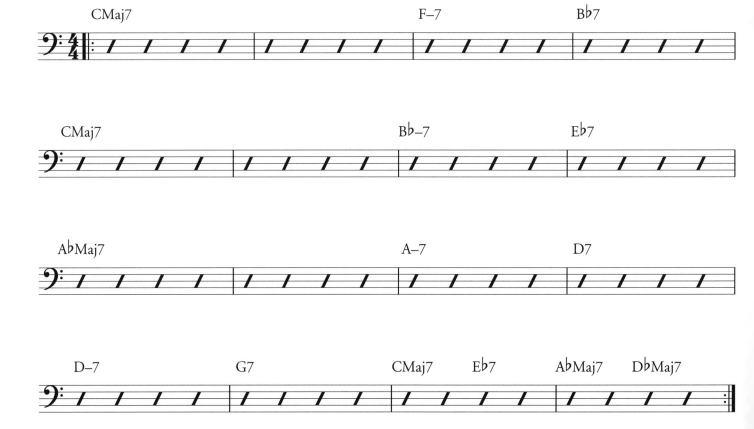

Simplify the Turnaround

You can simplify the turnaround in measures 15 and 16 by using just the E♭ triad, instead of E♭7, as written. Then, you can use C Phrygian for all chords of the turnaround. We will use E♭7 for this lesson.

Bass Lines

Practice this bass part along with the progression. Sing the roots as you play. What is this progression's pitch axis?

Practice Pads

Record a 30-second practice pad for each chord used in this progression: CMaj7, AbMaj7, Bb7, Eb7, D7, DbMaj7, F–7, Bb–7, A–7, and G7.

Analysis

The pitch axis for this progression is C. The chords yield four modes (C Ionian, C Aeolian, C Phrygian, C Lydian), which are built from six tetrachords (C major, C minor, C Phrygian, C Lydian, G major, G Phrygian).

Mode 1. C Ionian

The lower tetrachord is C major (CMaj7, D–7, G7). The upper tetrachord is G major (CMaj7, D–7, G7). Combined, these tetrachords form the C Ionian mode.

Mode 2. C Aeolian

The lower tetrachord is C minor (F–7, B♭, A♭Maj7). The upper tetrachord is G Phrygian (A♭Maj7, D♭Maj7, B♭–7, E♭7). Combined, these tetrachords form the C Aeolian mode.

Mode 3. C Phrygian

The lower tetrachord is C Phrygian (A♭Maj7, D♭Maj7, B♭–7, E♭7). The upper tetrachord is G Phrygian (A♭Maj7, D♭Maj7, B♭–7, E♭7, F–7, B♭7). Combined, these tetrachords form the C Phrygian mode.

Mode 4. C Lydian

The lower tetrachord is C Lydian (A–7, D7). The upper tetrachord is G major (CMaj7, D–7, G7, A–7, D7). Combined, these tetrachords form the C Lydian mode.

PRACTICE

Fingering

Warm up for improvising by practicing these tetrachord fingerings.

C Ionian

C Aeolian

C Phrygian

C Lydian

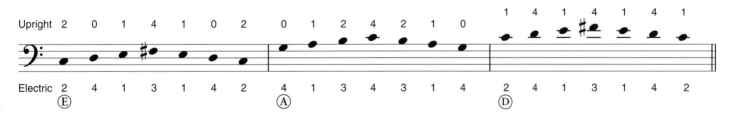

Pad Improvising

Improvise over each of your recorded chord pads. Practice the appropriate mode's tetrachords over each chord, as shown. Use just one tetrachord at a time, and repeat the pads so that you can use both tetrachords of the given mode. Listen for where the unstable notes resolve, for each chord. (Tetrachords in **bold** include notes that require special handling.)

Follow these steps for each pad:

1. Practice improvising in the lower tetrachord only. When you are ready to use the upper tetrachord, first play the note G.

2. Practice improvising in the upper tetrachord only. When you are ready to use the whole mode, first play the root of the pad.

3. Practice improvising while moving throughout the entire mode. End the exercise on the root of the pad.

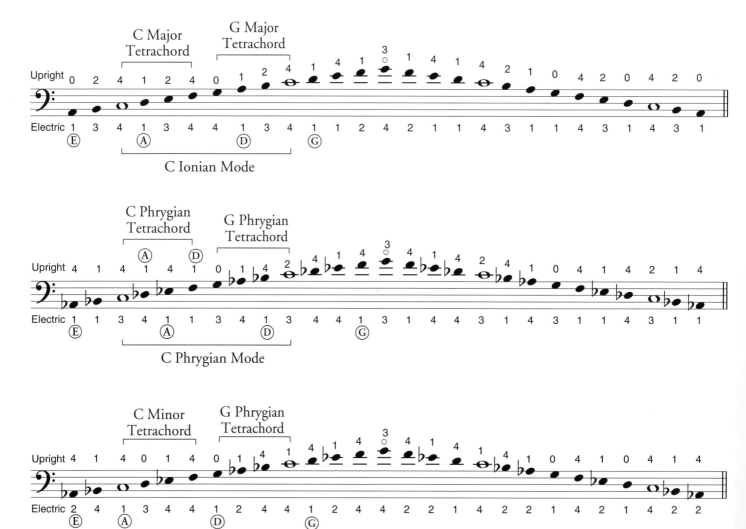

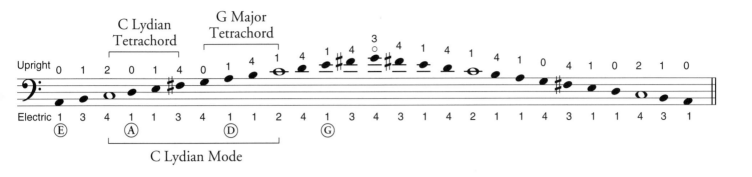

PITCH TENDENCIES FOR PRACTICE PADS

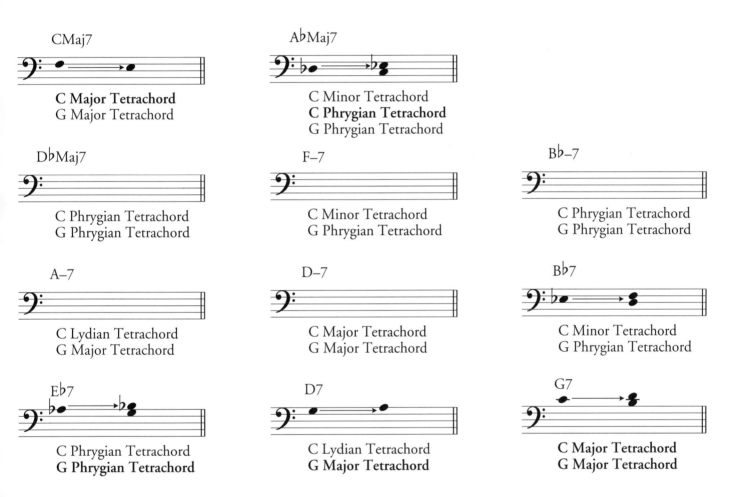

Tetrachord Practice

Improvise over the chord progression, using the appropriate tetrachord over each chord. Practice using each tetrachord in all octaves. Then try this exercise while reading the chord progression at the beginning of this lesson, without the tetrachords labeled.

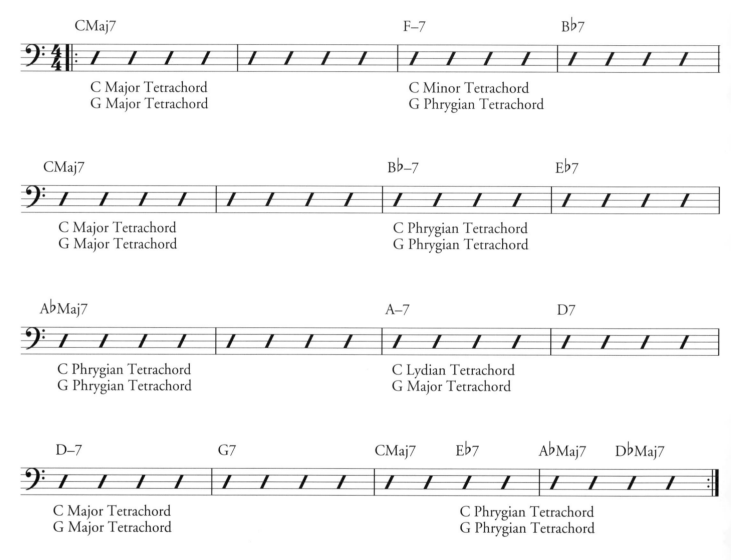

Mode Practice

Play the written half notes along with the recording. Continue the pattern, choosing
the correct half note for each harmony you encounter.

Continue...

Mixed-Rhythm Modal Exercise

Next, play this mixed-rhythm exercise. Again, listen to the sound of the notes against each chord. Continue cycling through the modes, and use rhythm to control stable and unstable notes. Notice the use of quarter-note triplets; this rhythm can be very effective when soloing.

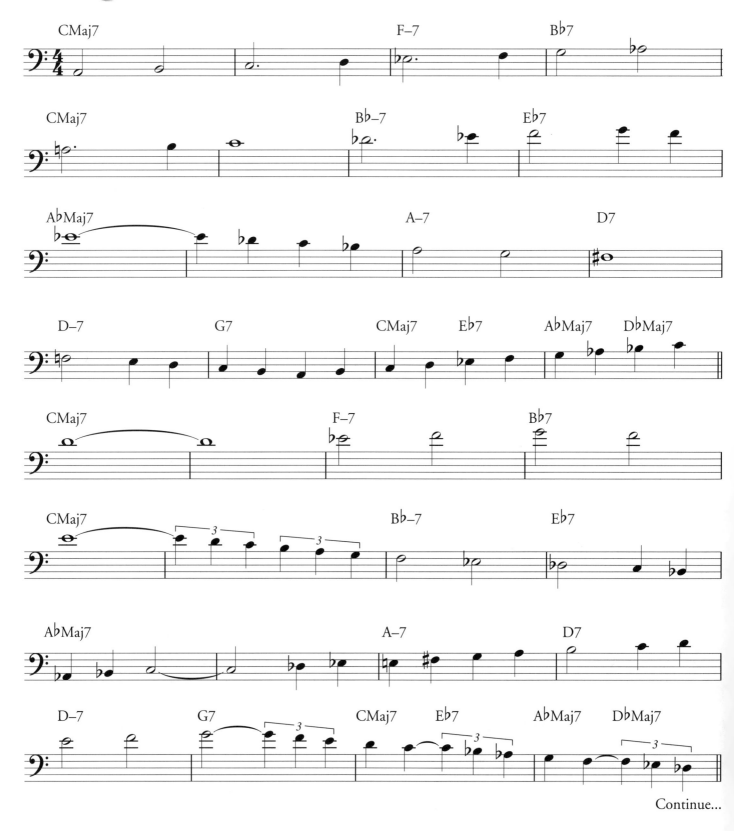

Continue...

PERFORMANCE

Etude

Practice this etude along with the recording, track 18, singing it as you play. Analyze its use of tetrachords and modes, and notice how the unstable notes resolve. It is demonstrated on track 19.

Solo

1. Improvise a solo over the "Lady Bird" changes. When you're comfortable with this progression, record your solo.

2. Transcribe the best two choruses of your improvised solo, and rewrite them as you see fit.

3. Practice playing this final solo along with the recording, using it to lead into further improvisations.

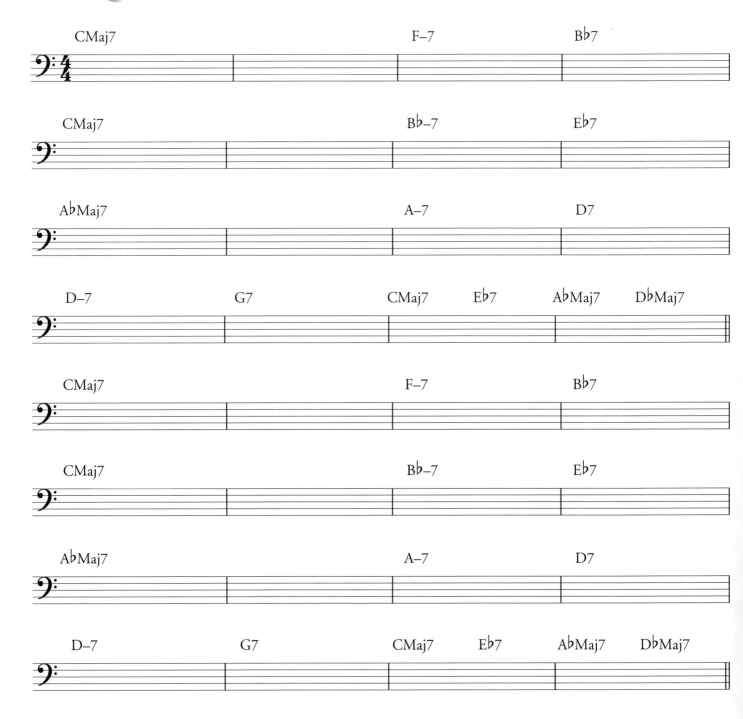

Lesson 12. Five Modes

This lesson is based on "Just Friends," by John Klemmer and Sam M. Lewis.

GETTING ORIENTED

Listen to this progression. Play and sing the chord roots along with the recording.

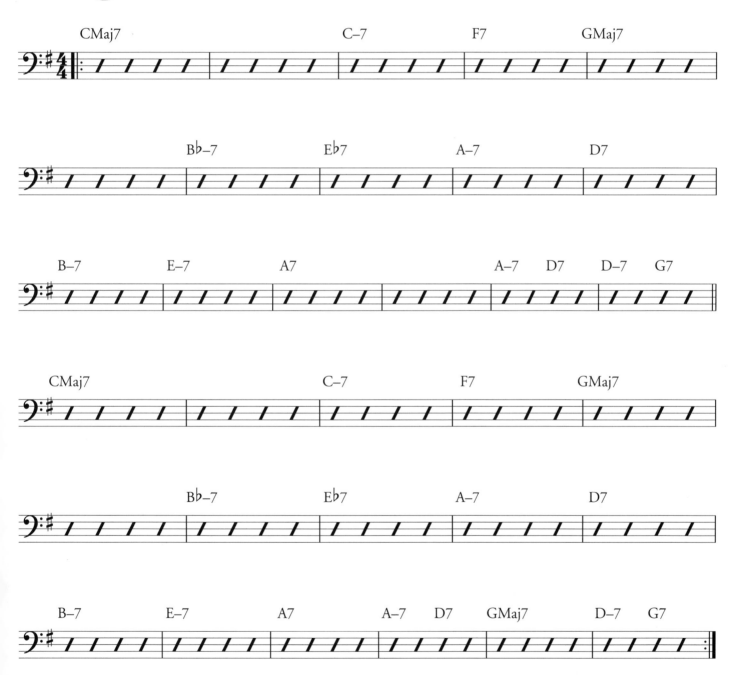

Bass Lines

Practice this bass part along with the progression. What is this progression's pitch axis?

Analyzing This Tune

This progression is a little tricky to analyze because it starts on the IVMaj7 chord. When beginning your analysis, it's often helpful to look at the progression's key signature and its ending chord, as a way to get oriented to the progression's tonal center.

Practice Pads

Record a 30-second practice pad for each chord used in this progression: GMaj7, CMaj7, C–7, B♭–7, A–7, B–7, E–7, D–7, F7, E♭7, D7, A7, and G7.

Analysis

The pitch axis for this progression is G. The chords yield five modes (G Mixolydian, G Aeolian, G Ionian, G Locrian, and G Lydian), which are built from eight tetrachords (G major, G minor, G Phrygian, G Lydian, D major, D minor, D Phrygian, and D♭ Lydian).

Mode 1. G Ionian

The lower tetrachord is G major (GMaj7, CMaj7, A–7, B–7, D–7, E–7, D7, G7). The upper tetrachord is D major (GMaj7, CMaj7, A–7, D7, B–7, E–7, A7). Combined, these tetrachords form the G Ionian mode.

Mode 2. G Aeolian

The lower tetrachord is G minor (C–7, F7). The upper tetrachord is D Phrygian (C–7, F7). Combined, these tetrachords form the G Aeolian mode.

Mode 3. G Mixolydian

The lower tetrachord is G major (GMaj7, CMaj7, A–7, B–7, D–7, E–7, D7, G7). The upper tetrachord is D minor (D–7, G7). Combined, these tetrachords form the G Mixolydian mode.

Mode 4. G Locrian

The lower tetrachord is G Phrygian (B♭–7, E♭7). The upper tetrachord is D♭ Lydian (B♭–7, E♭7). Combined, these tetrachords form the G Locrian mode.

Mode 5. G Lydian

The lower tetrachord is G Lydian (A7). The upper tetrachord is D major (GMaj7, CMaj7, A–7, D7, B–7, E–7, A7). Combined, these tetrachords form the G Lydian mode.

PRACTICE

Fingering

Warm up for improvising by practicing these tetrachord fingerings.

G Ionian

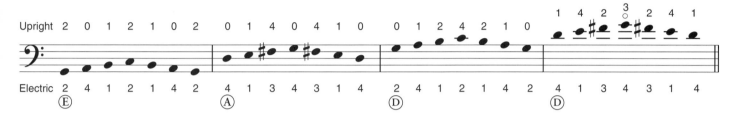

G Aeolian

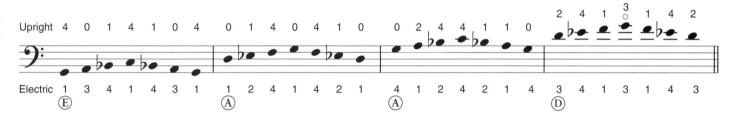

G Locrian

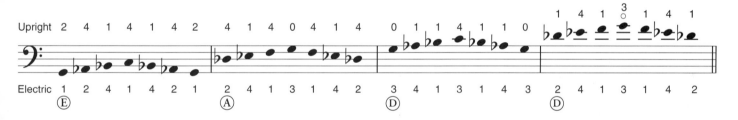

G Lydian

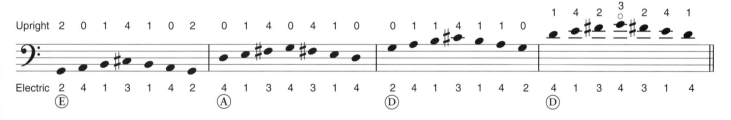

G Mixolydian

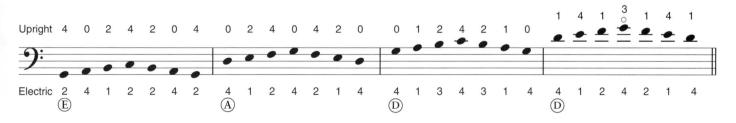

Pad Improvising

Improvise over each of your recorded chord pads. Practice the appropriate mode's tetrachords over each chord, as shown. Use just one tetrachord at a time, and repeat the pads so that you can use both tetrachords of the given mode. Listen for where the unstable notes resolve, for each chord. (Tetrachords in **bold** include notes that require special handling.)

Follow these steps for each pad:

1. Practice improvising in the lower tetrachord only. When you are ready to use the upper tetrachord, first play the note D.

2. Practice improvising in the upper tetrachord only. When you are ready to use the whole mode, first play the root of the pad.

3. Practice improvising while moving throughout the entire mode. End the exercise on the root of the pad.

> ### G Locrian
>
> When you're practicing G Locrian over B♭–7 and E♭7, remember that the upper tetrachord begins on a D♭, rather than a D♮.

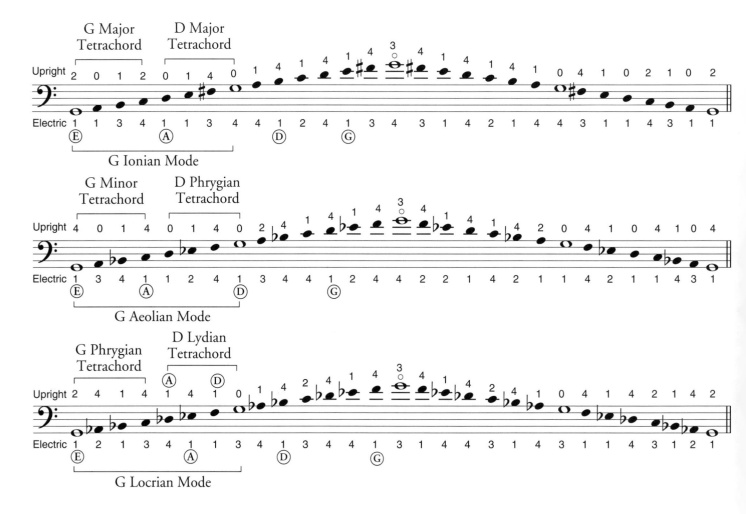

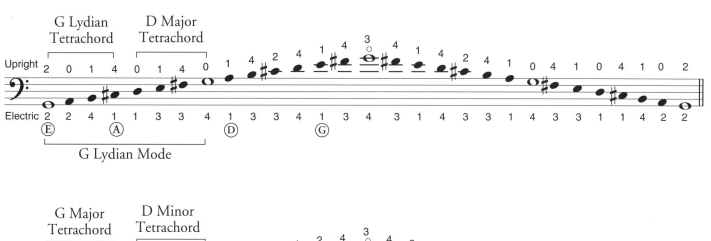

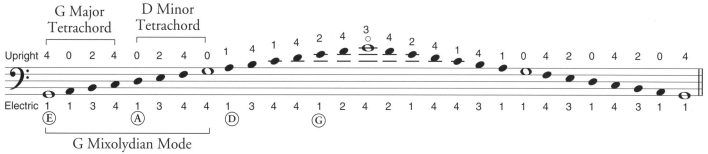

PITCH TENDENCIES FOR PRACTICE PADS

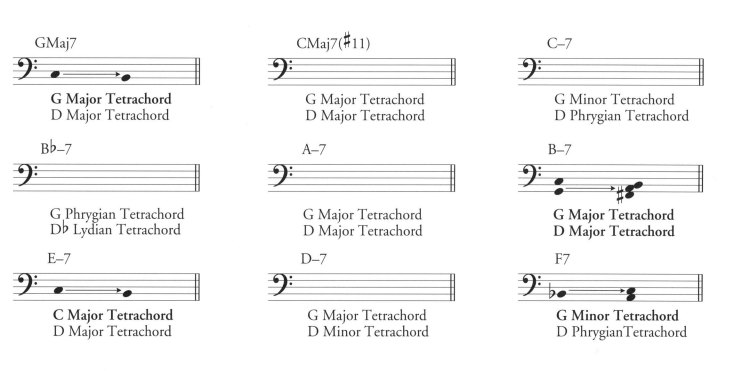

GMaj7

G Major Tetrachord
D Major Tetrachord

CMaj7(♯11)

G Major Tetrachord
D Major Tetrachord

C–7

G Minor Tetrachord
D Phrygian Tetrachord

B♭–7

G Phrygian Tetrachord
D♭ Lydian Tetrachord

A–7

G Major Tetrachord
D Major Tetrachord

B–7

G Major Tetrachord
D Major Tetrachord

E–7

C Major Tetrachord
D Major Tetrachord

D–7

G Major Tetrachord
D Minor Tetrachord

F7

G Minor Tetrachord
D PhrygianTetrachord

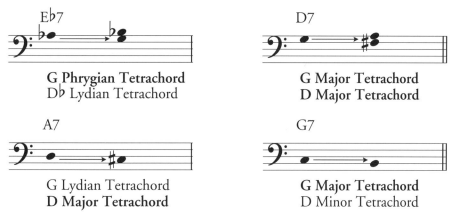

E♭7

G Phrygian Tetrachord
D♭ Lydian Tetrachord

D7

G Major Tetrachord
D Major Tetrachord

A7

G Lydian Tetrachord
D Major Tetrachord

G7

G Major Tetrachord
D Minor Tetrachord

Tetrachord Practice

Improvise over the chord progression, using the appropriate tetrachord over each chord. Practice using each tetrachord in all octaves. Then try this exercise while reading the chord progression at the beginning of this lesson, without the tetrachords labeled.

Mode Practice

Play the written half notes along with the recording. Continue the pattern, choosing the correct half note for each harmony you encounter.

Continue...

Mixed-Rhythm Modal Exercise

Next, play this mixed-rhythm exercise. Again, listen to the sound of the notes against each chord. Continue cycling through the modes, and use rhythm to control stable and unstable notes.

Continue...

PERFORMANCE

Etude

Practice this etude along with the recording, track 20, singing it as you play. Analyze its use of tetrachords and modes, and notice how the unstable notes resolve. It is demonstrated on track 21.

Solo

1. Improvise a solo over the "Just Friends" changes. When you're comfortable with this progression, record your solo.

2. Transcribe the best chorus of your improvised solo, and rewrite it as you see fit.

3. Practice playing this final solo along with the recording, using it to lead into further improvisations.

What's Next?

In this method, we have emphasized the relationship between notes, chords, tetrachords, and modes. When you are comfortable with these techniques, you will find that you've developed a linear approach to improvising that is an essential element of any well-constructed solo. Your soloing will be more meaningful and expessive, with your every note and melodic shape directly related to the progression's underlying harmony. This mastery is a tremendous accomplishment, and it will help you to become a more expressive musician.

The next step is to apply these techniques to different transpositions of the progressions in this book, and then to apply them to new progressions. Follow the approach that we used in these lessons.

- ❏ Begin by listening to the progression and playing a bass line to the changes, to get them into your ears and fingers.

- ❏ Analyze the progression. What are the modes and tetrachords implied by the harmony? What's the pitch axis? Can one pitch axis be established for the entire progression, or will the progression require more than one pitch axis?

- ❏ Make a recording of pads for yourself, for each of the progression's chords, and practice improvising with tetrachords and modes over each pad. Which pitches require special handling? Where do they naturally resolve? Save the pads from these lessons. They can be used for practicing many ideas. Also, visit our Web site for more pads at www.playingthechanges.com

- ❏ Practice improvising over the form, first by isolating each tetrachord, then by using each entire mode, as appropriate. Record, transcribe, and improve your solos.

- ❏ Transcribe other people's solos for that tune.

Finally, you will be able to improvise without thinking too much about the theory, and to "pre-hear" where our lines are going. You will develop a sense of phrasing that comes from controlling the stable and unstable notes. Use this to build well-constructed, meaningful solos.

Berklee Press has a few other titles that might interest you, in your pursuit of improvisation and creative music making. Try these:

The Bass Player's Handbook, by Greg Mooter

Modern Jazz Voicings, by Ted Pease and Ken Pullig

Reharmonization Techniques, by Randy Felts

Be sure to visit our Web site at www.playingthechanges.com for free additional materials for this method.

I hope that you found this book helpful. Drop me a line at Berklee Press (information@berkleepress.com), and tell me how it's going.

—Paul Del Nero

About the Author

Bassist Paul Del Nero is Associate Professor of Ear Training at Berklee College of Music. The concepts in this book come from the curriculum he developed for Berklee's Performance Ear Training courses. They have been used to train thousands of students to improvise.

Paul is an active performer, recording artist, educator, and clinician. He has performed internationally on acoustic and electric bass, with small groups and big bands, in festivals, clubs, and shows, and on radio and television. Artists he has performed with include Hal Crook, Charlie Rouse, James Williams, Hal Galper, Donald Byrd, Junior Mance, Mose Allison, Jimmy Guiffre, Buddy Tate, Benny Golson, and Bob Moses. Record labels he has

recorded with include Concord, Candid, and GM. Jazz festival appearances include Vienne, Toulon, Berlin, Los Angeles, and New York. He was Artist in Residence at The Banff Centre.

Paul is a recipient of the USIA Grant under the American Cultural Specialist Program. He holds a bachelor of music from Berklee and a master's from New England Conservatory of Music.

The Berklee Press Bass Line...

AS SERIOUS ABOUT MUSIC AS YOU ARE

Playing the Changes: Bass
A Linear Approach to Improvising
By Paul Del Nero

| ISBN: 0-634-02222-9 | HL: 50449510 | BOOK/CD $19.95 |

Explore the possibilities of focused and linear improvisation, and develop your ability to create musically effective melodies with greater freedom and depth of expression.

Instant Bass
By Danny Morris

| ISBN: 0-634-01667-9 | HL: 50449502 | BOOK/CD $14.95 |

Berklee's revolutionary series to get you jammin' right away. Simple lessons and the play-along CD give you just enough technique and theory to get you playing.

Slap Bass Lines
By Joe Santerre   ≣TAB INCLUDED≣

| ISBN: 0-634-02144-3 | HL: 50449508 | BOOK/CD $19.95 |

Learn the art of creating solid slap bass grooves in rock, funk, and jazz music, with more than 80 examples of slap bass lines to learn.

Chord Studies for Electric Bass
By Rich Appleman and Joseph Viola

| ISBN: 0-634-01646-6 | HL: 50449750 | BOOK $14.95 |

Great for intermediate to advanced players, this book develops all aspects of bass technique, including basic and extended chords in all keys.

Essential Rock Grooves for Bass
Featuring Danny Morris

| ISBN:0-87639-037-8 | HL: 50448019 | DVD $19.95 |

Study the techniques to help you anchor your band with a solid foundation of bass lines, chord progressions, and rhythmic and harmonic variations.

Berklee Practice Method: Bass
By Rich Appleman and John Reppuci

| ISBN: 0-634-00650-9 | HL: 50449427 | BOOK/CD $14.95 |

The first-ever method developed to help teach musicians how to play in a band. The book and play-along CD will help you improve your timing, technique, and reading ability.

Blues Improvisation Complete:
C Bass Instruments
By Jeff Harrington

| ISBN: 0-634-01532-X | HL: 50449488 | BOOK/CD $19.95 |

Learn to improvise in jazz, Latin, fusion, blues, and rock styles with musical examples and play-along CD.

A Guide to Jazz Improvisation:
Bass Clef
By John LaPorta

| ISBN:0-634-00764-5 | HL: 50449443 | BOOK/CD $16.95 |

Includes ear and rhythm training with call-and-response and play-along with legendary jazz artists on included CD.

Afro-Cuban Slap Bass Lines
By Oscar Stagnaro

| ISBN: 0-634-02378-0 | HL: 50449512 | BOOK/CD $19.95 |

Learn to play bass in seven popular Afro-Cuban styles. The included CD has percussion tracks, play-along tracks, and complete songs.

Rock Bass Lines
By Joe Santerre   ≣TAB INCLUDED≣

| ISBN: 0-634-01432-3 | HL: 50449478 | BOOK/CD $19.95 |

Contains tons of riffs and lines found in your favorite rock tunes. Play along with the killer tracks in eight different rock styles on the included CD.

Bass Player's Handbook
By Greg Mooter

| ISBN: 0-634-02300-4 | HL: 50449511 | BOOK $24.95 |

Provides bassists with a complete guide to understanding the origins and works of their instrument.

Reading Contemporary Electric Bass
By Rich Appleman

| ISBN: 0-634-01338-6 | HL: 50449770 | BOOK $14.95 |

A comprehensive collection of exercises and performance studies designed to enable you to play in a wide range of musical styles.

Berklee Press books and DVDs are available wherever music books are sold.
Go to www.berkleepress.com or call 866-BERKLEE (237-5533) for a complete catalog of Berklee Press products.

DISTRIBUTED BY

HAL•LEONARD®